JUNE 50 COLORING PAGES
FOR OLDER KIDS RELAXATION

SHIH CHIEN HUA

PUBLISHED BY:
SHIH CHIEN HUA
Copyright © 2018

SEABIRD SHOP >50FOR

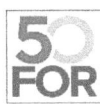

FB FAN PAGE

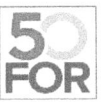

Disclaimer

The information contained in this book is for general information purposes only. The information is provided by the authors and while we endeavor to keep the information up to date and correct, we make no representations or warranties of any kind, express or implied, about the completeness, accuracy, reliability, suitability or availability with respect to the book or the information, products, services, or related graphics contained in the book for any purpose. Any reliance you place on such information is therefore strictly at your own risk.

JUNE 1ST

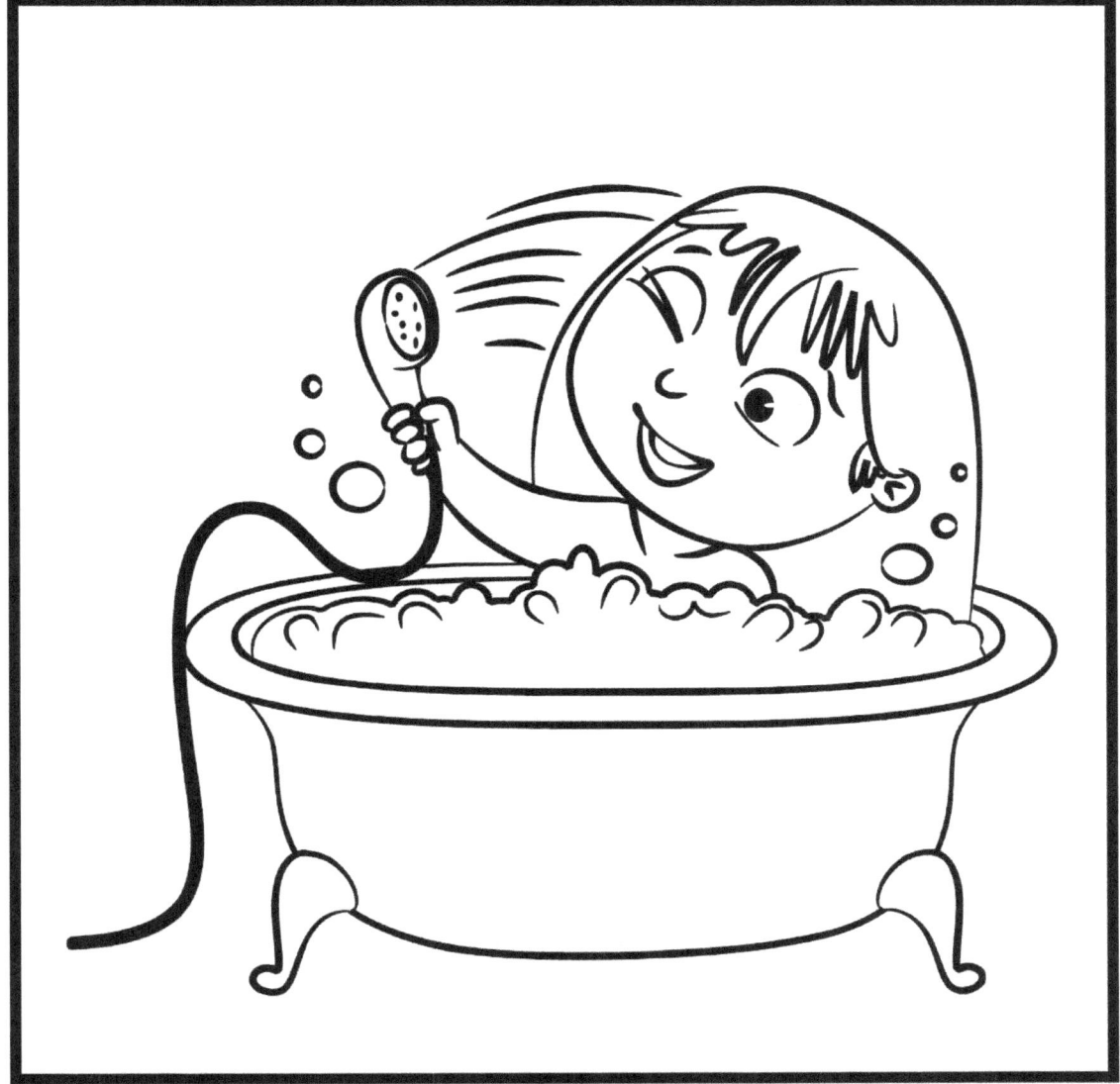

note:

_____

_____

_____

JUNE 2ND

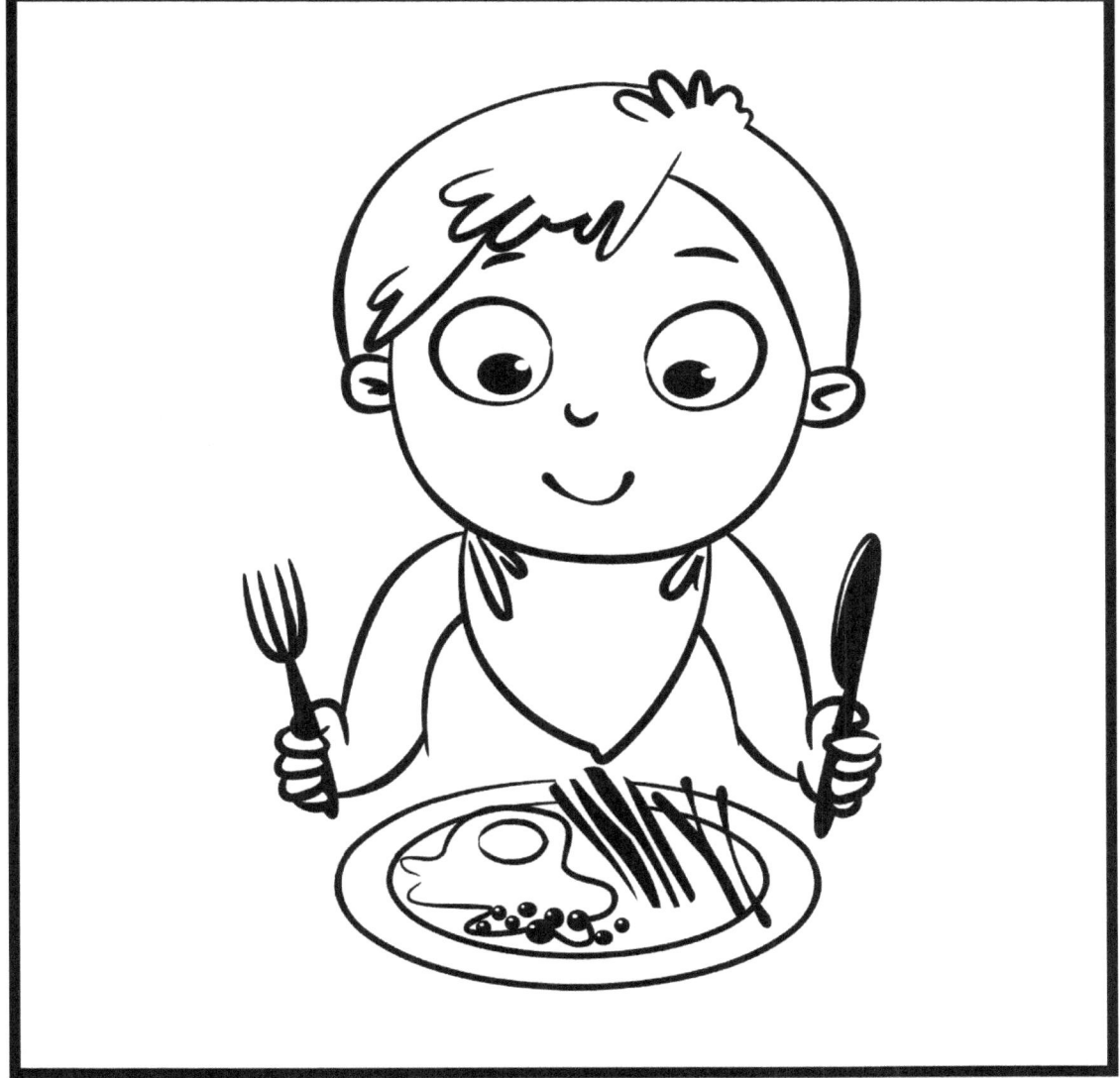

note:

_____

_____

_____

JUNE 3RD

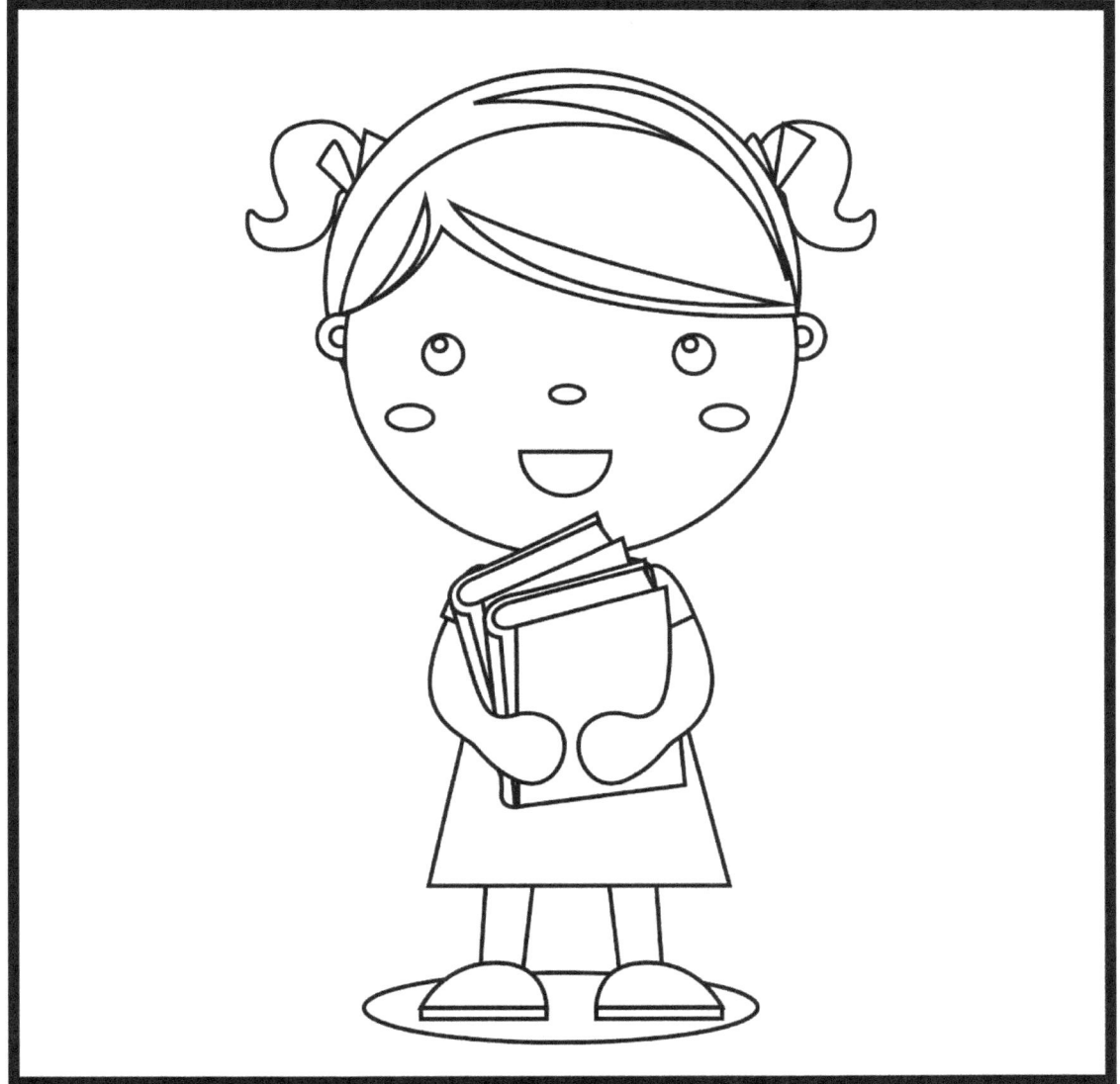

note:

_____

_____

_____

JUNE 4TH

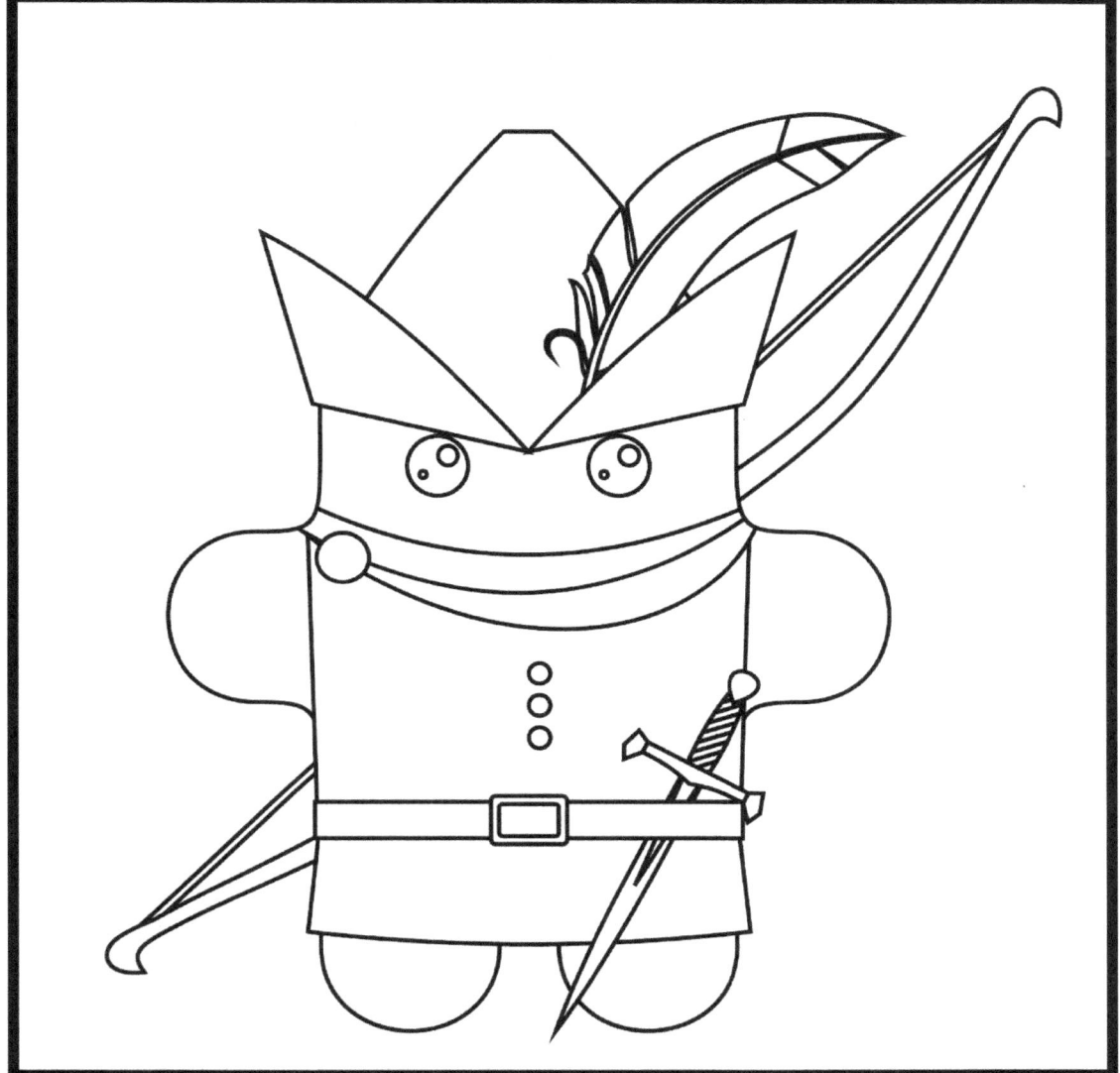

note:

_____

_____

_____

JUNE 5TH

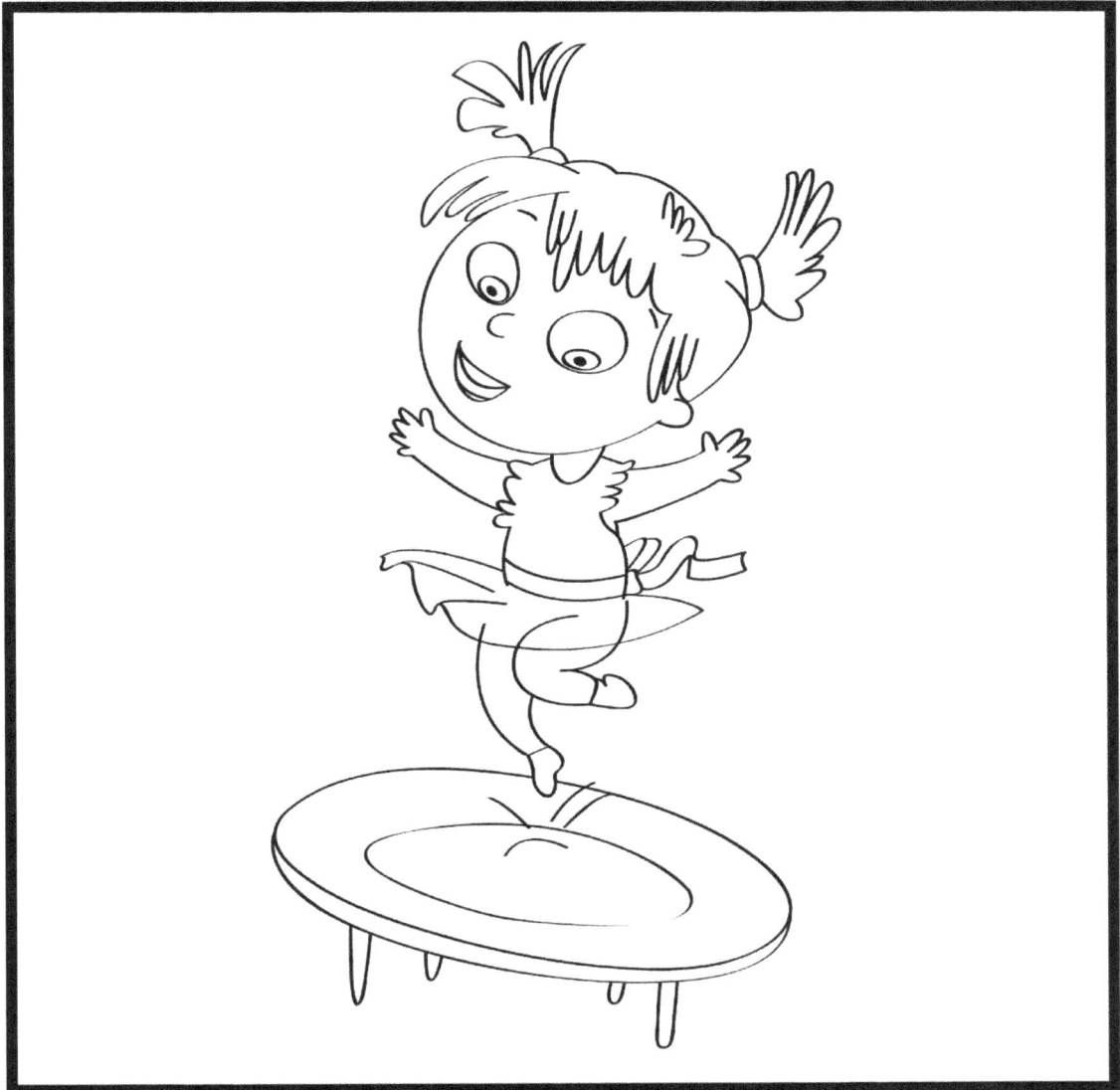

note:

_____

_____

_____

JUNE 6TH

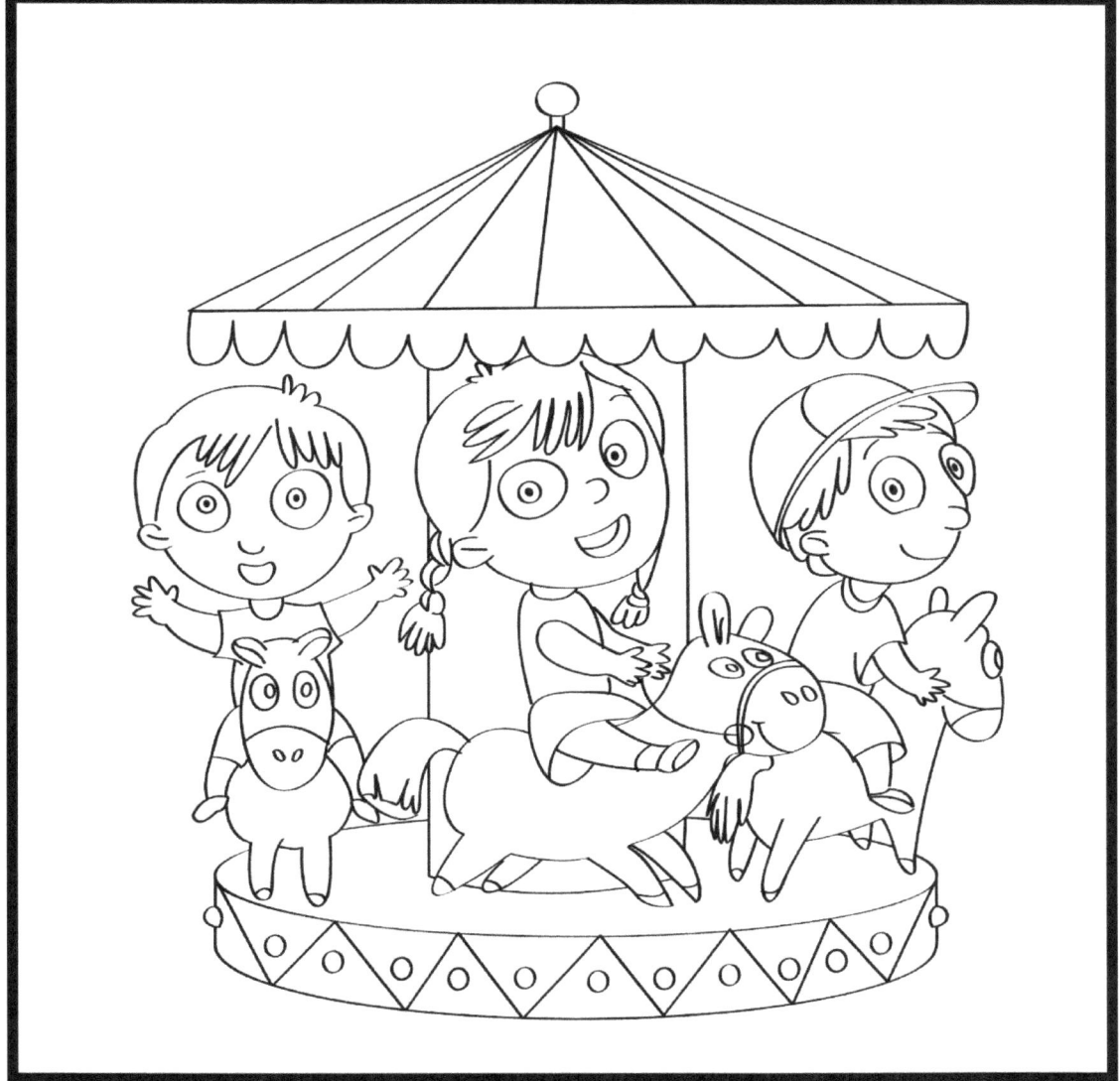

note:

_____

_____

_____

JUNE 7TH

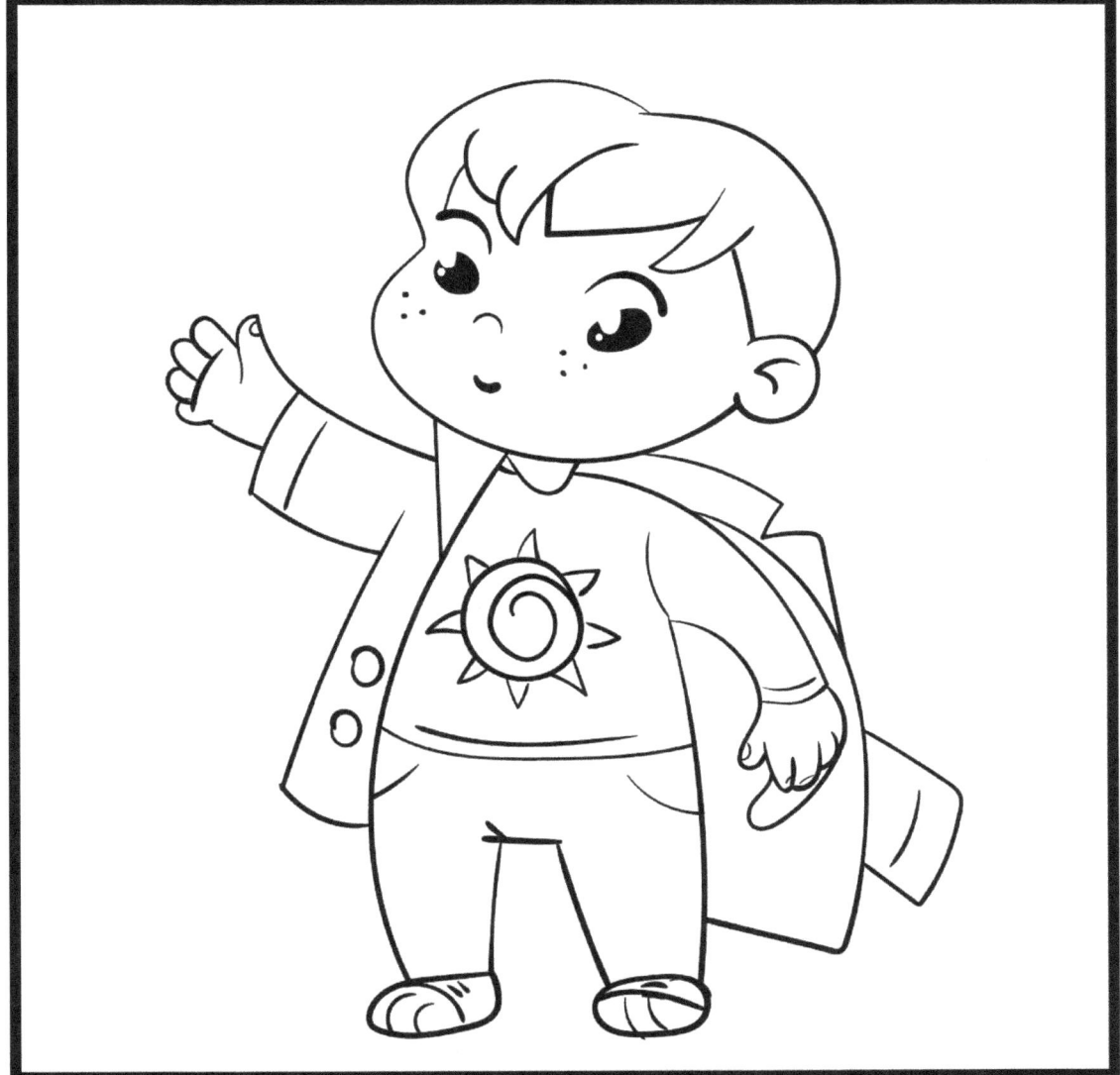

note:

_____

_____

_____

JUNE 8TH

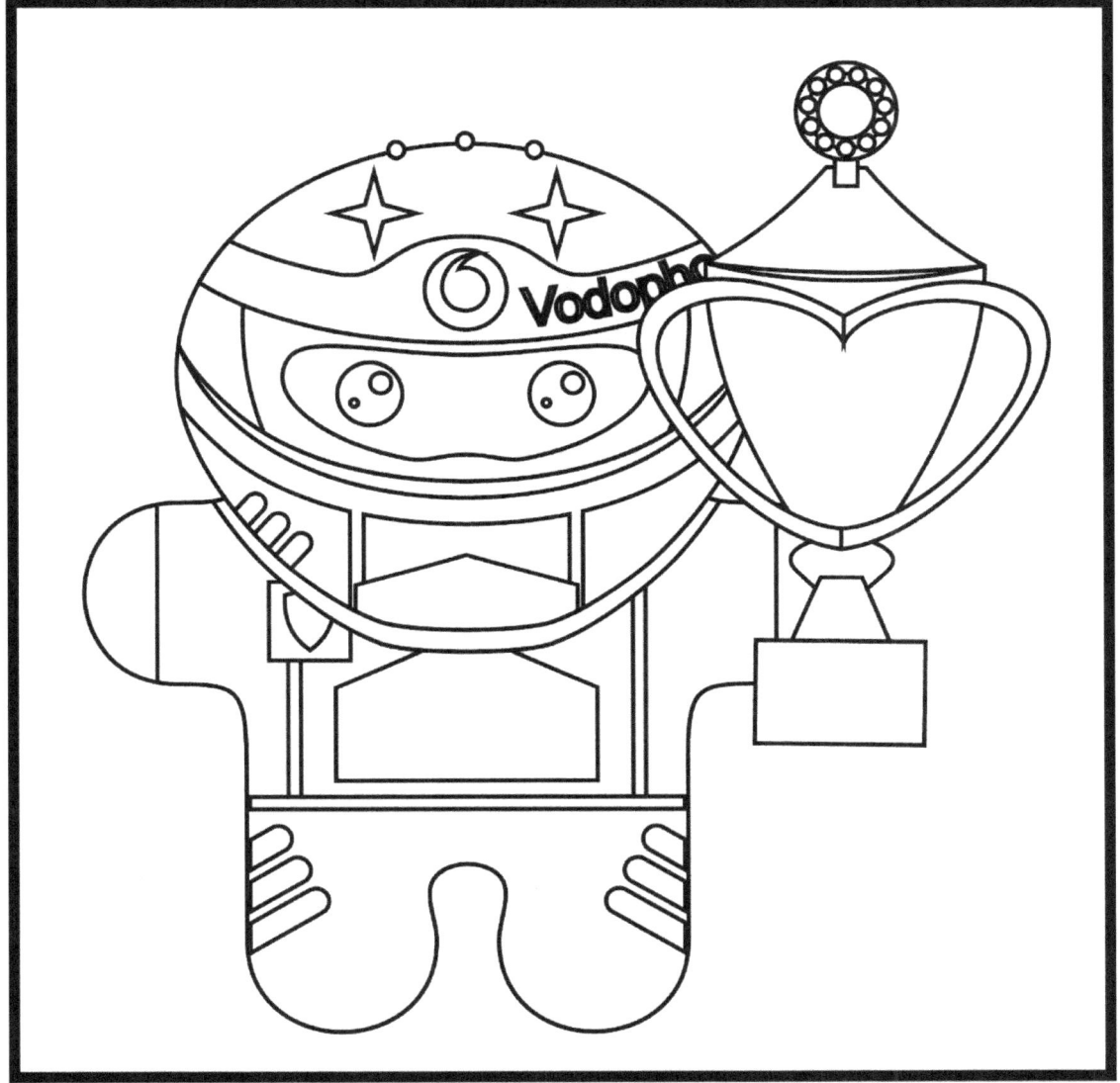

note:

_____

_____

_____

JUNE 9TH

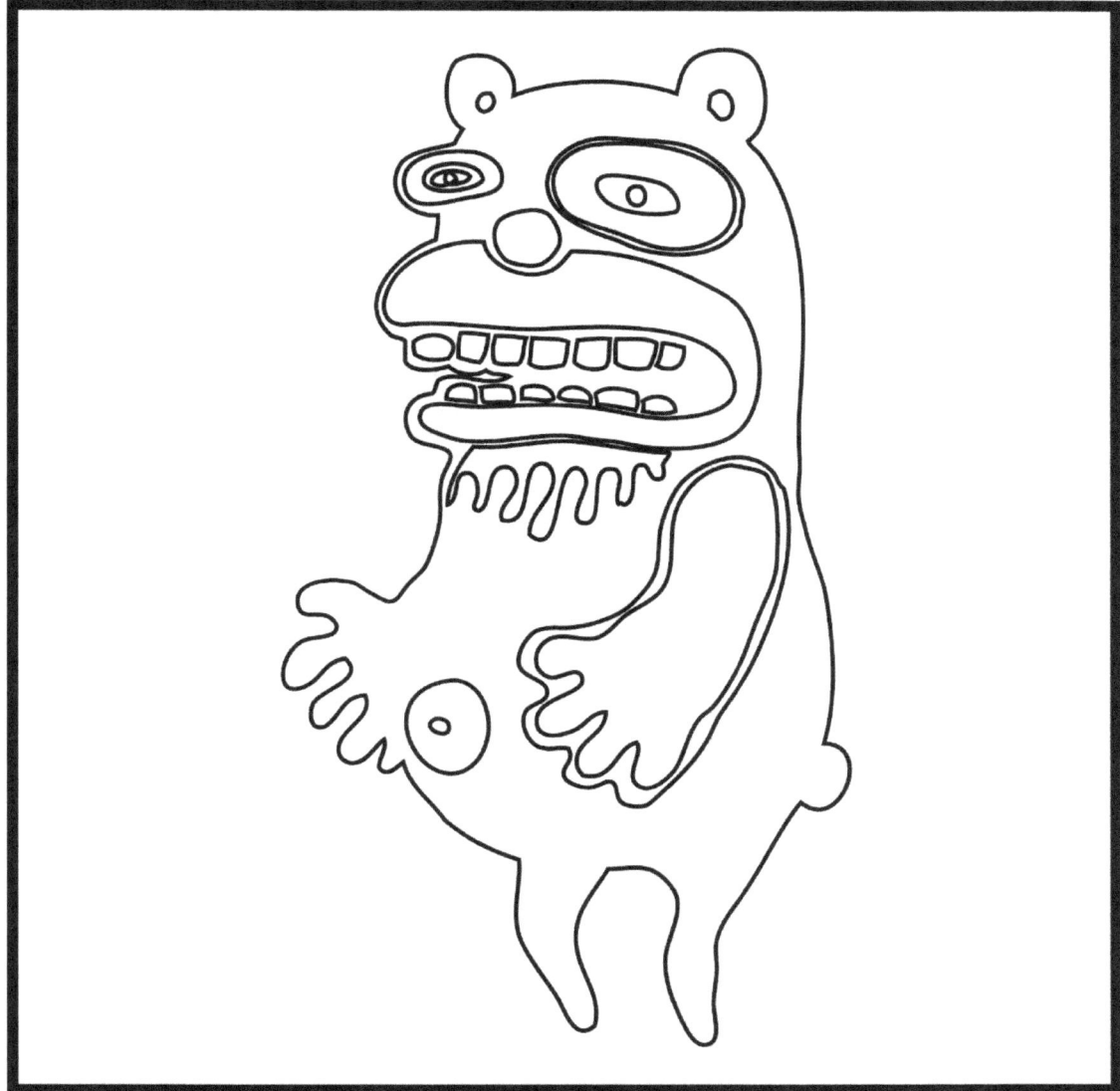

note:

_____

_____

_____

JUNE 10TH

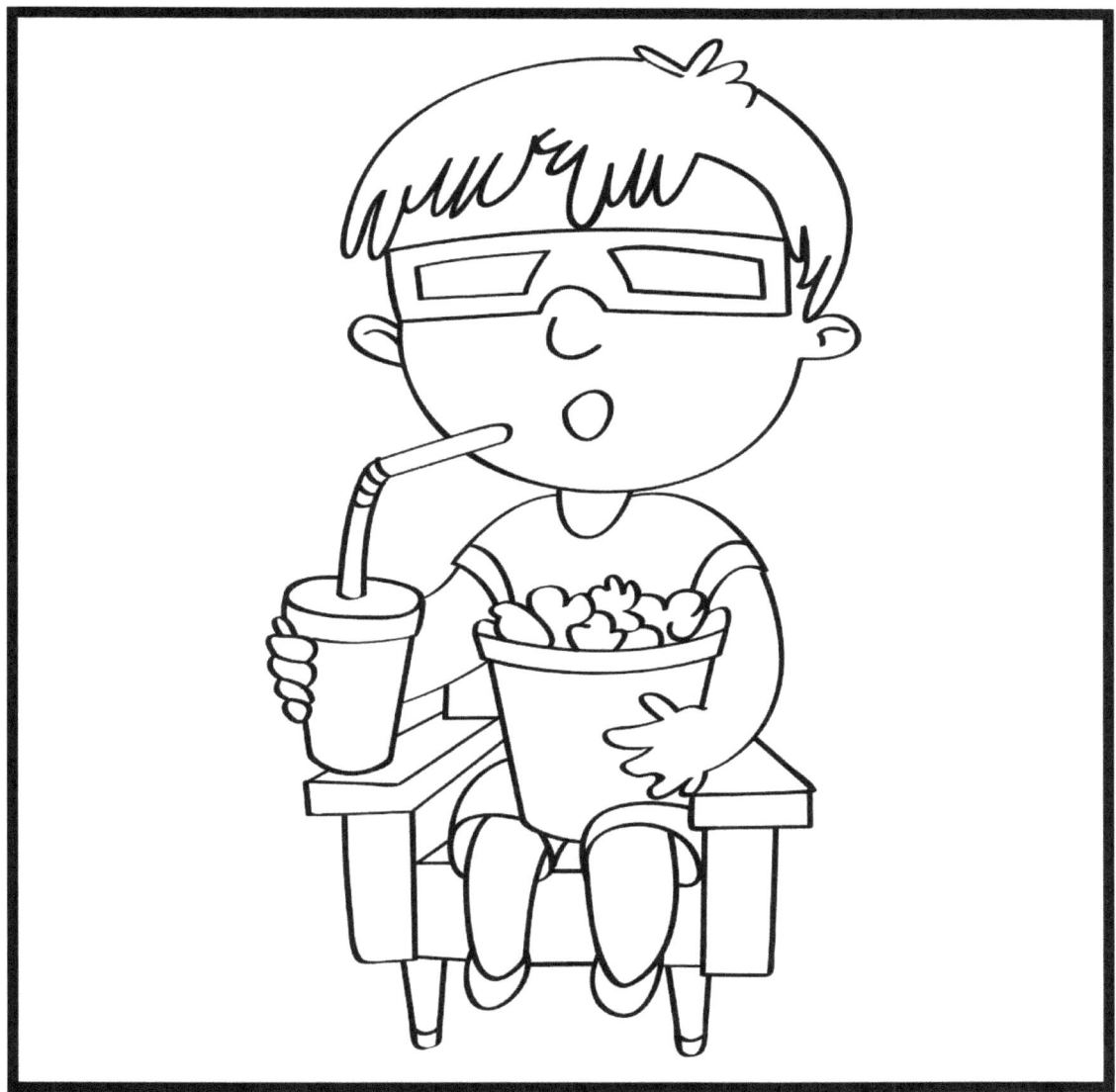

note:

_____

_____

_____

JUNE 11TH

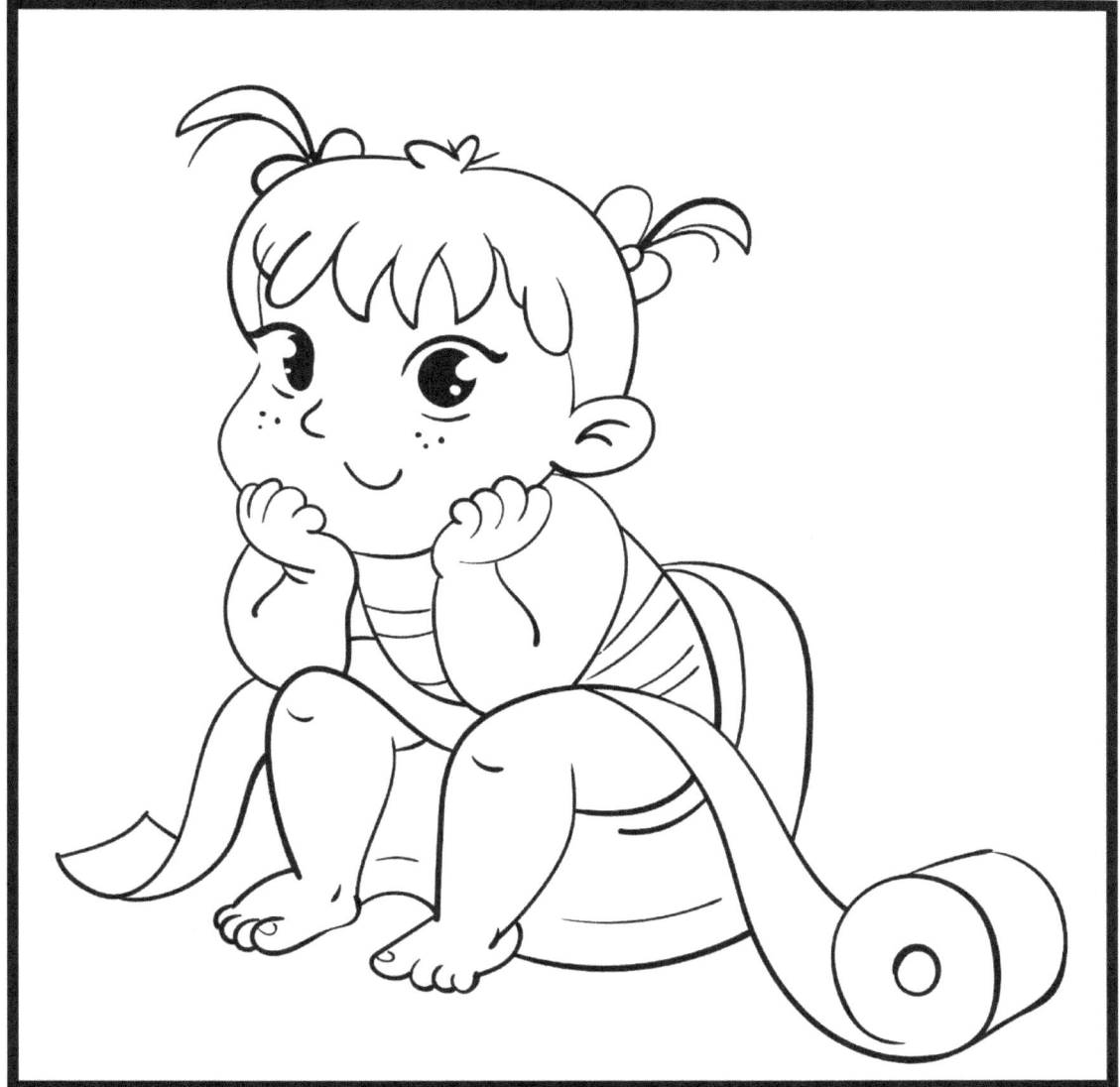

note:

_____

_____

_____

JUNE 12TH

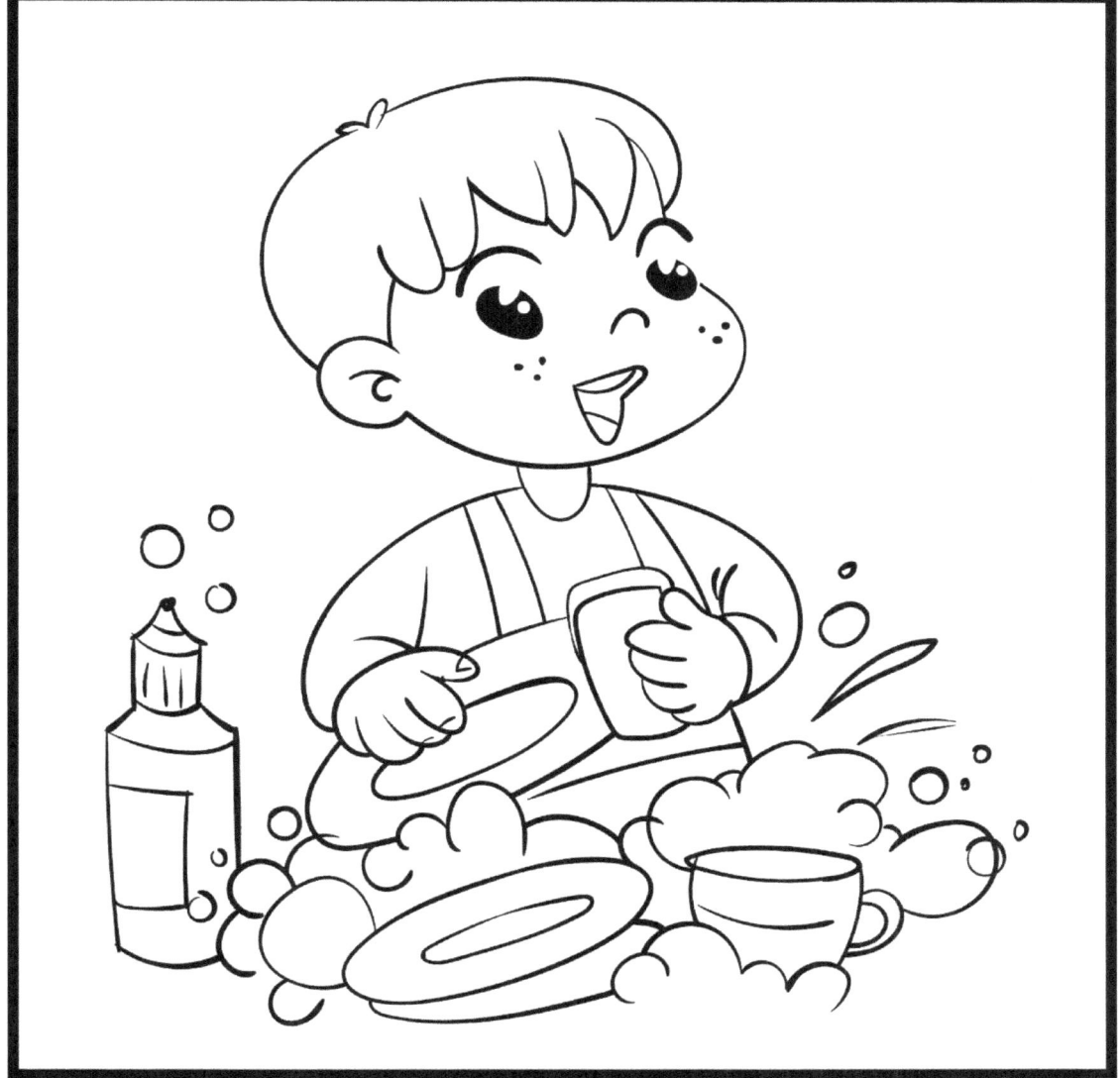

note:

_____

_____

_____

JUNE 13TH

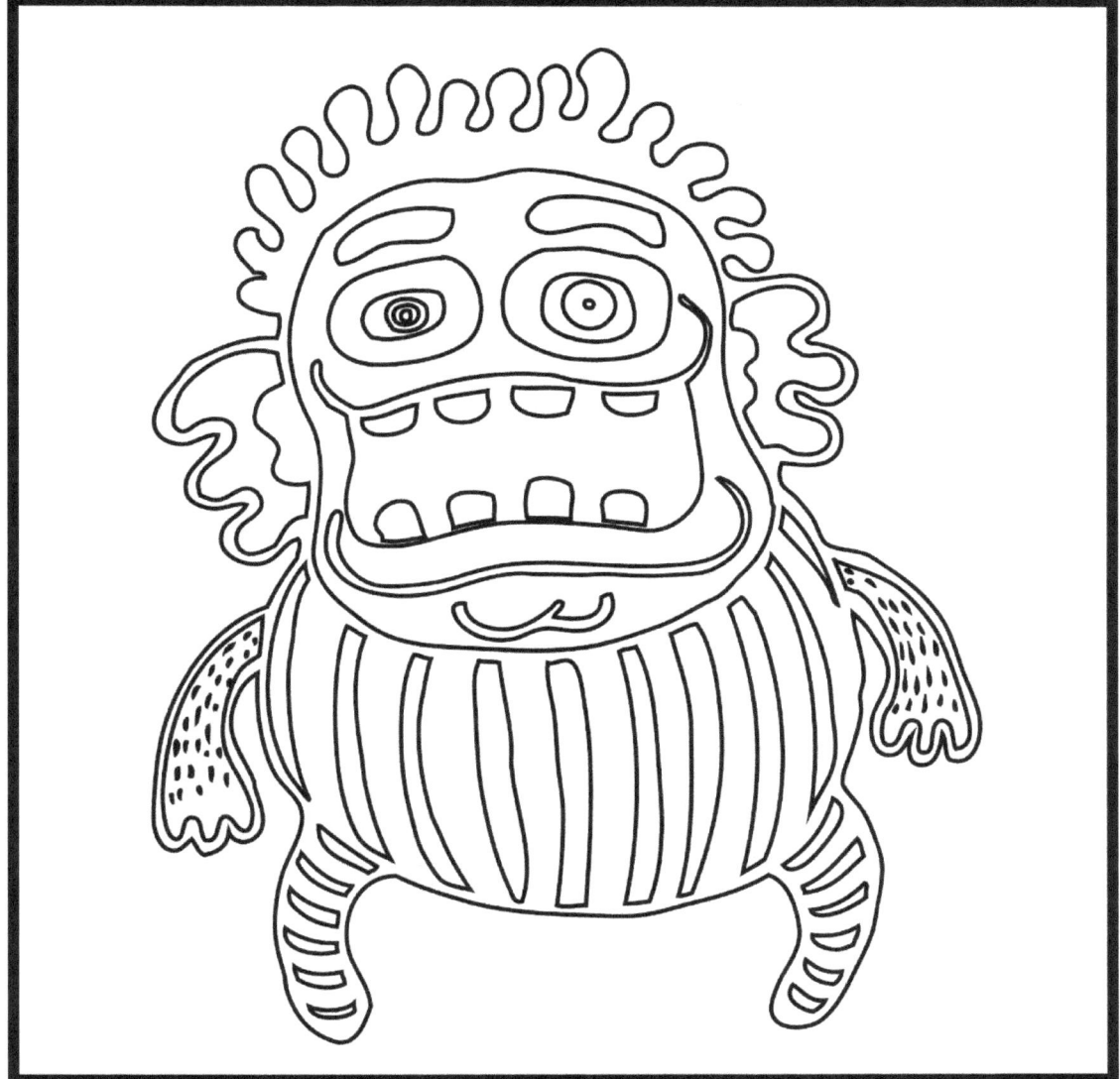

note:

_____

_____

_____

JUNE 14TH

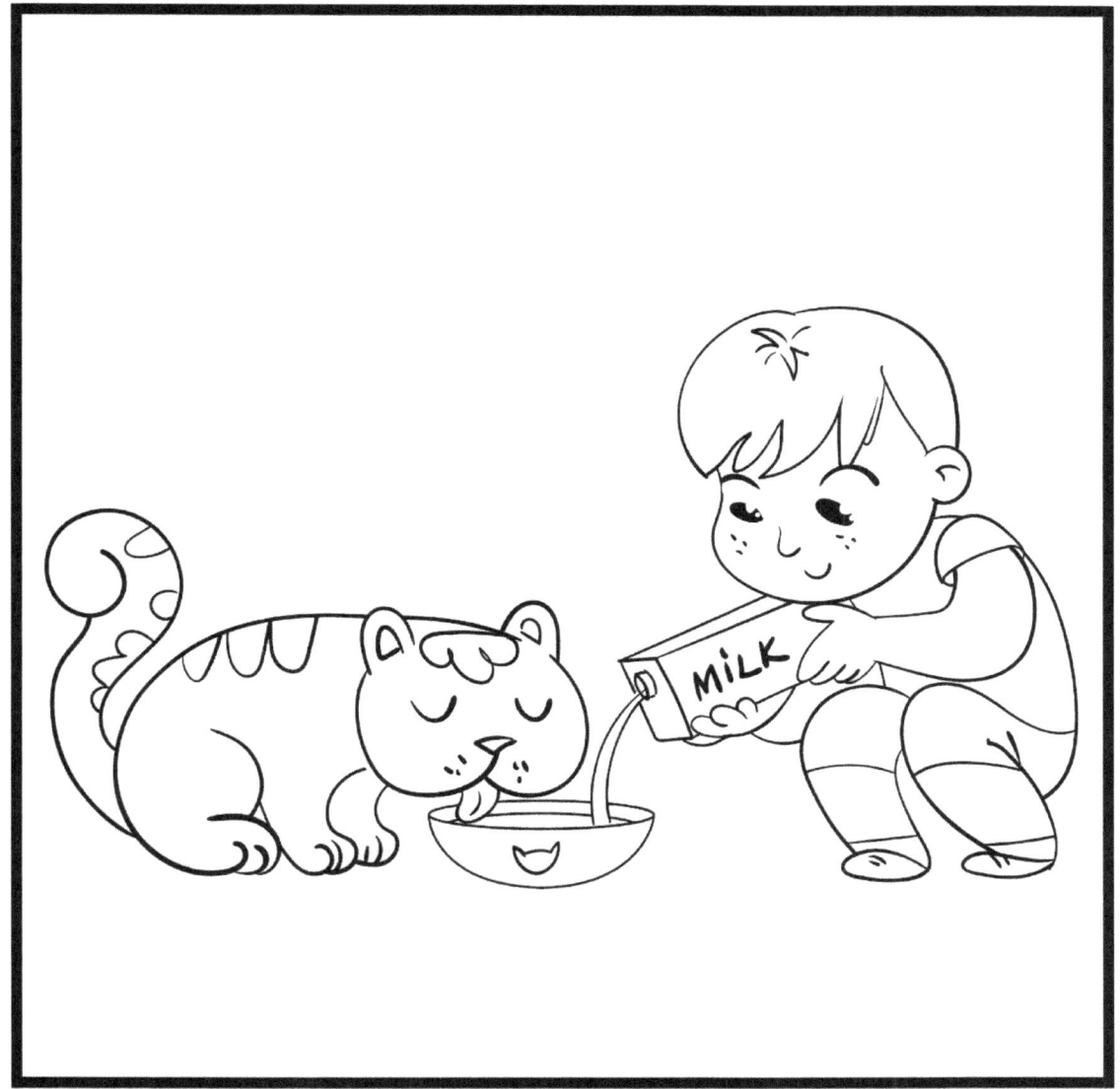

note:

_____

_____

_____

JUNE 15TH

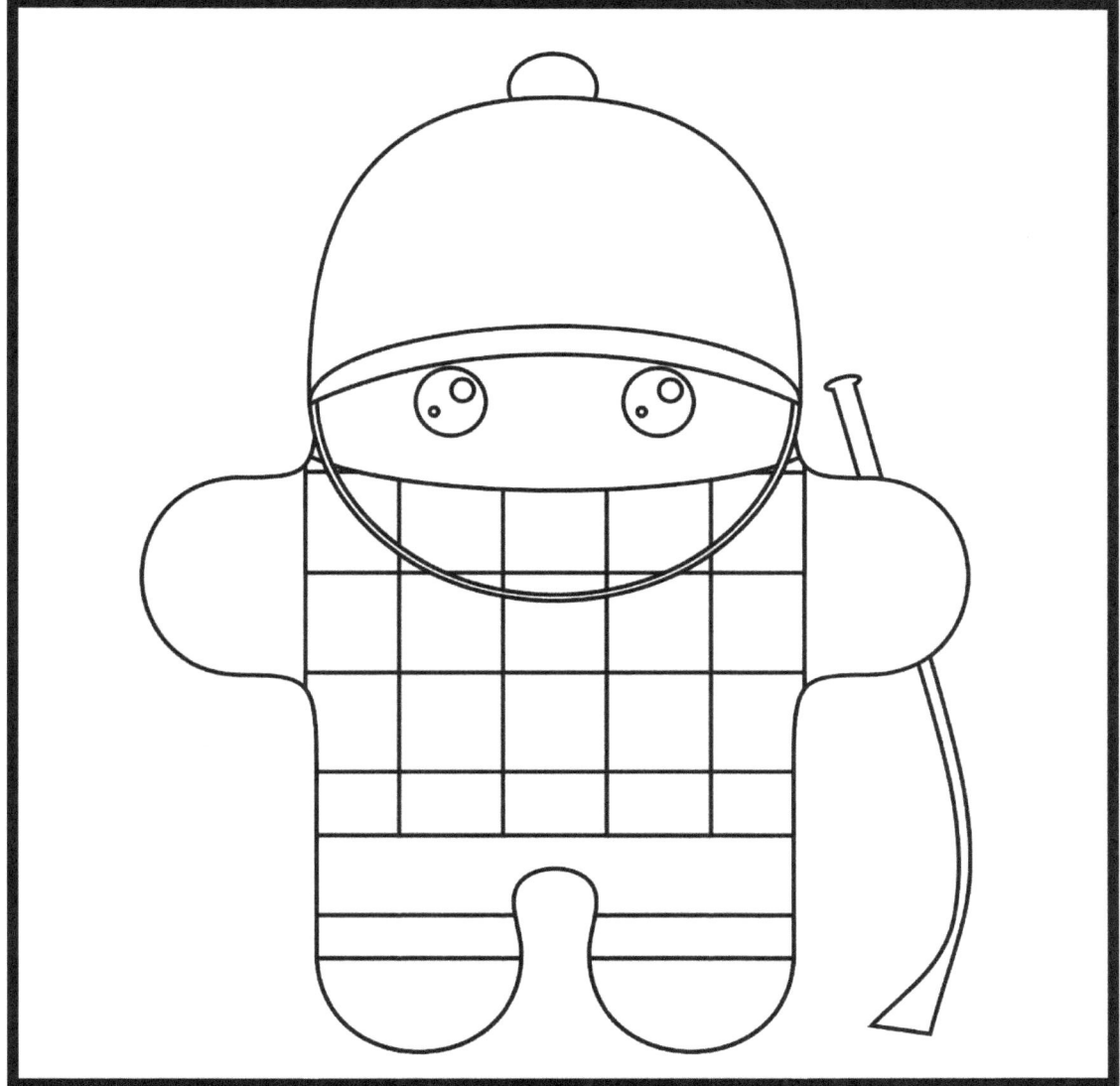

note:

_____

_____

_____

JUNE 16TH

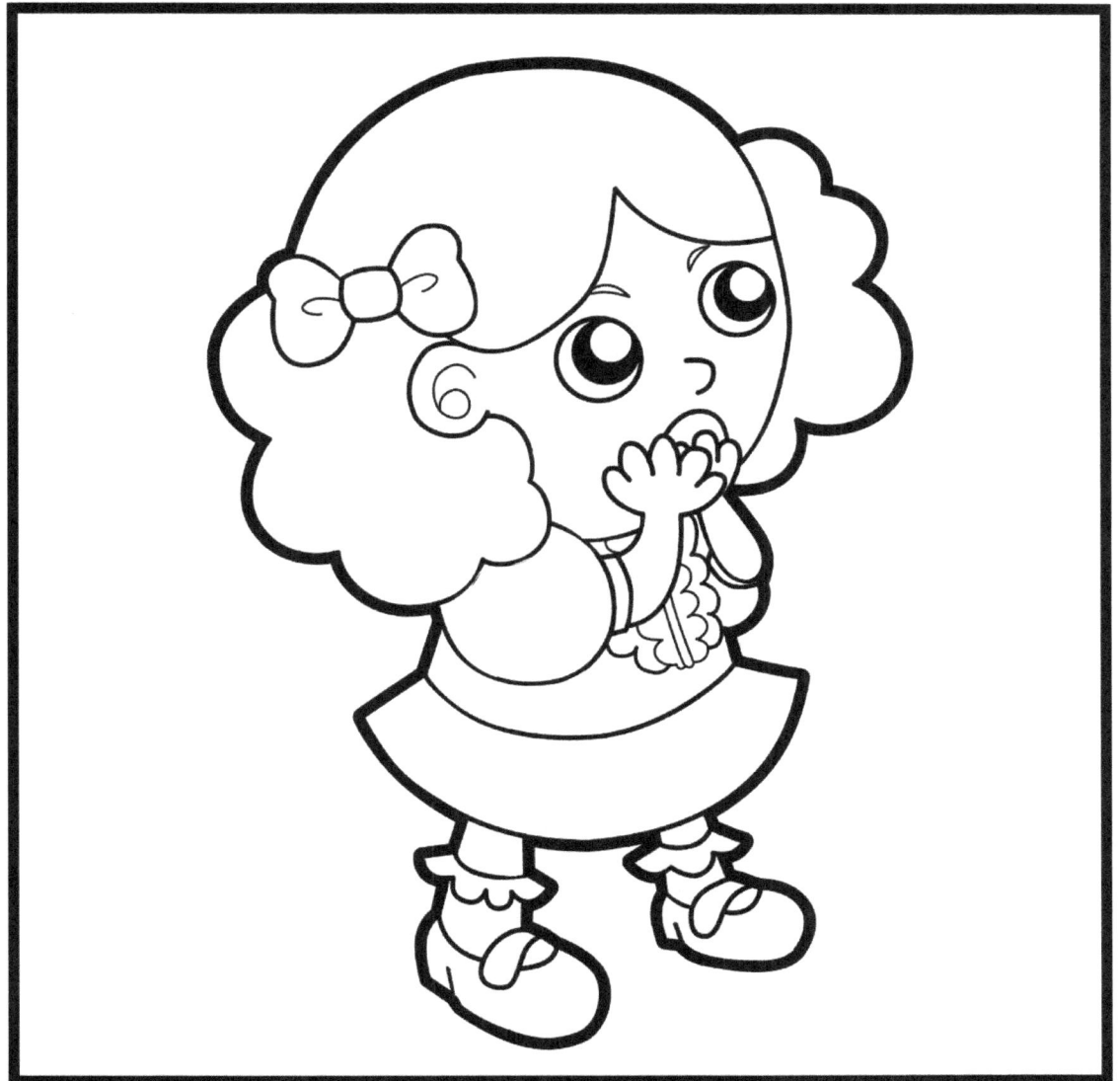

note:

_____

_____

_____

JUNE 17TH

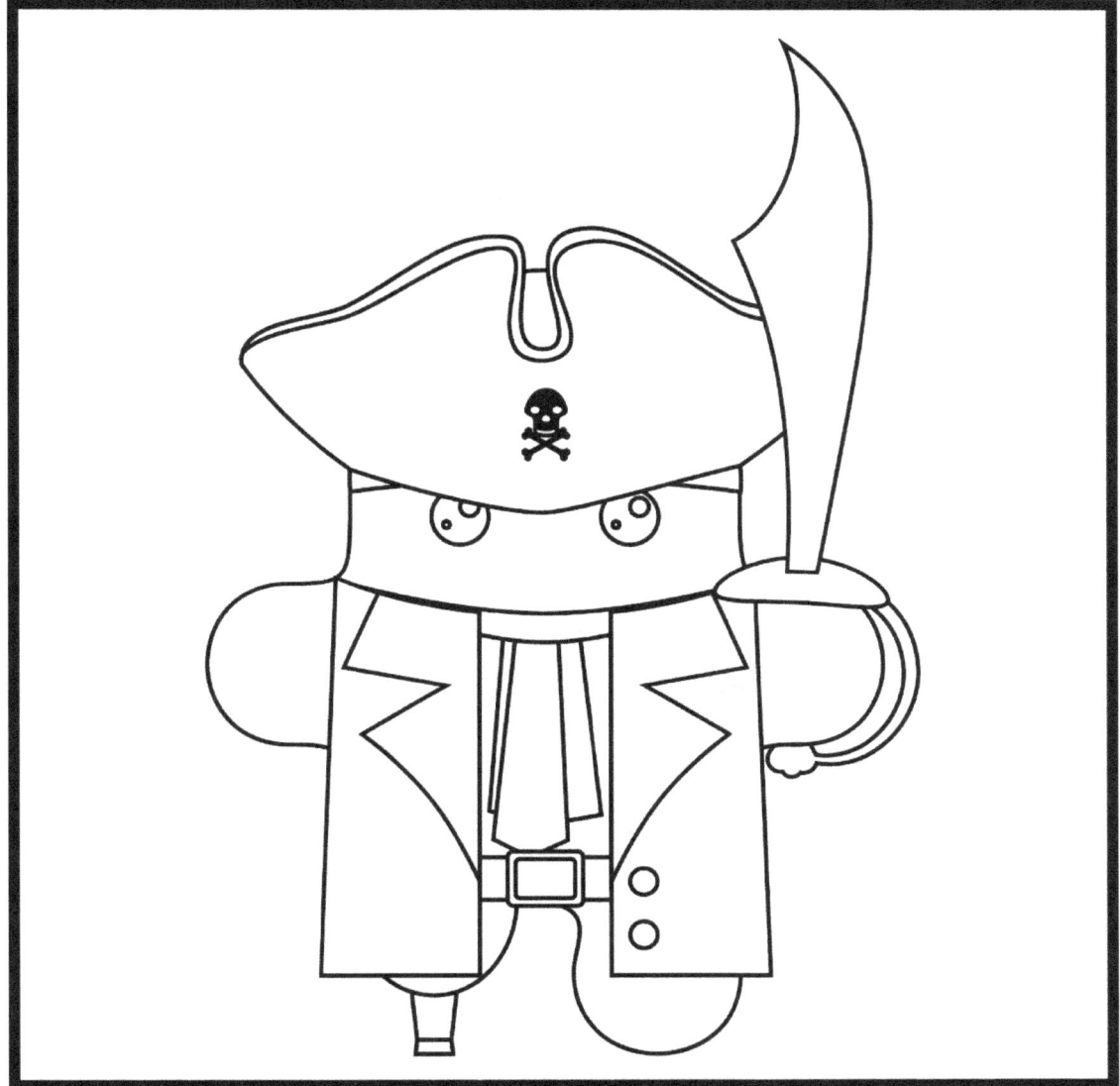

note:

_____

_____

_____

JUNE 18TH

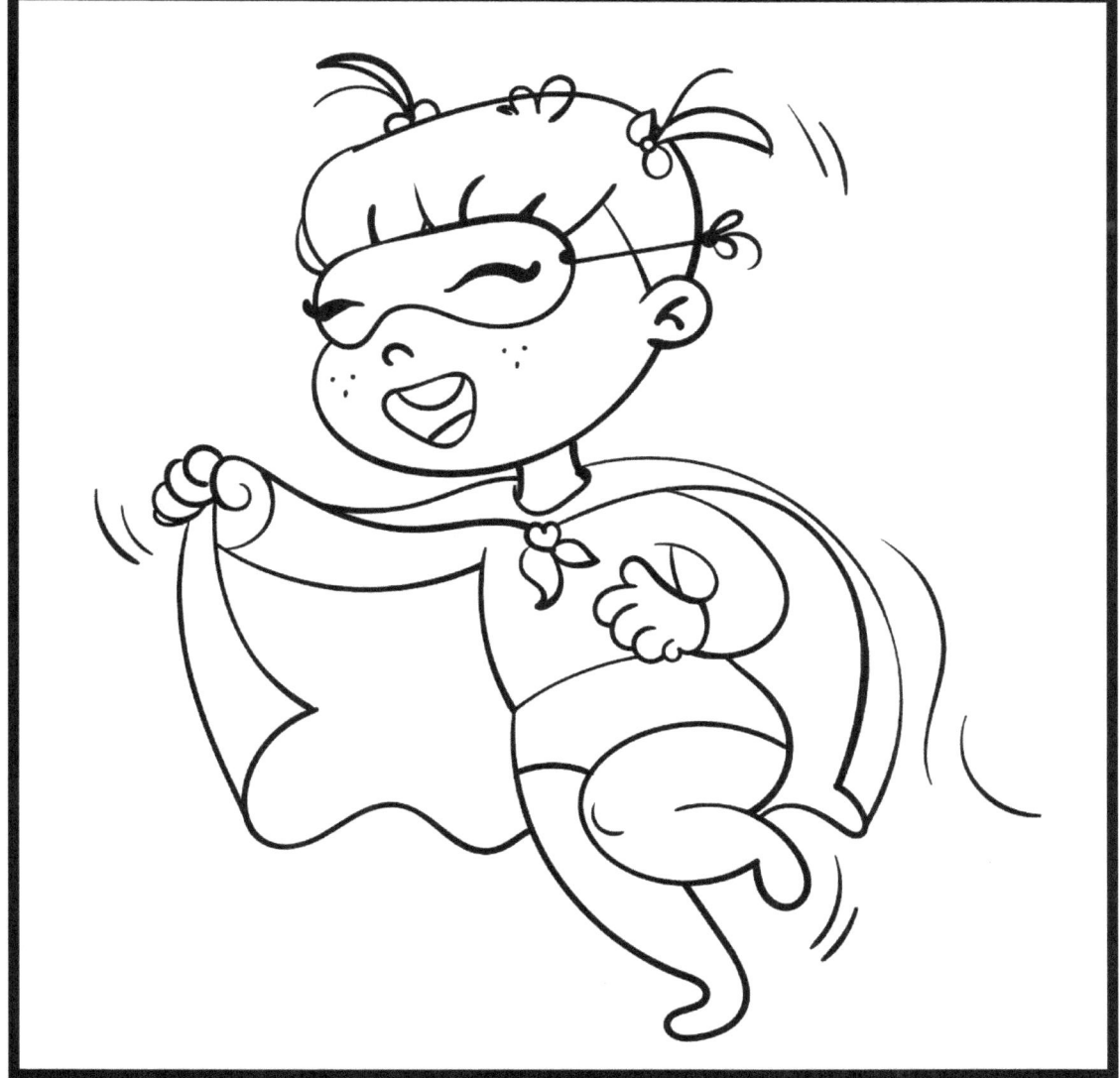

note:

_____

_____

_____

JUNE 19TH

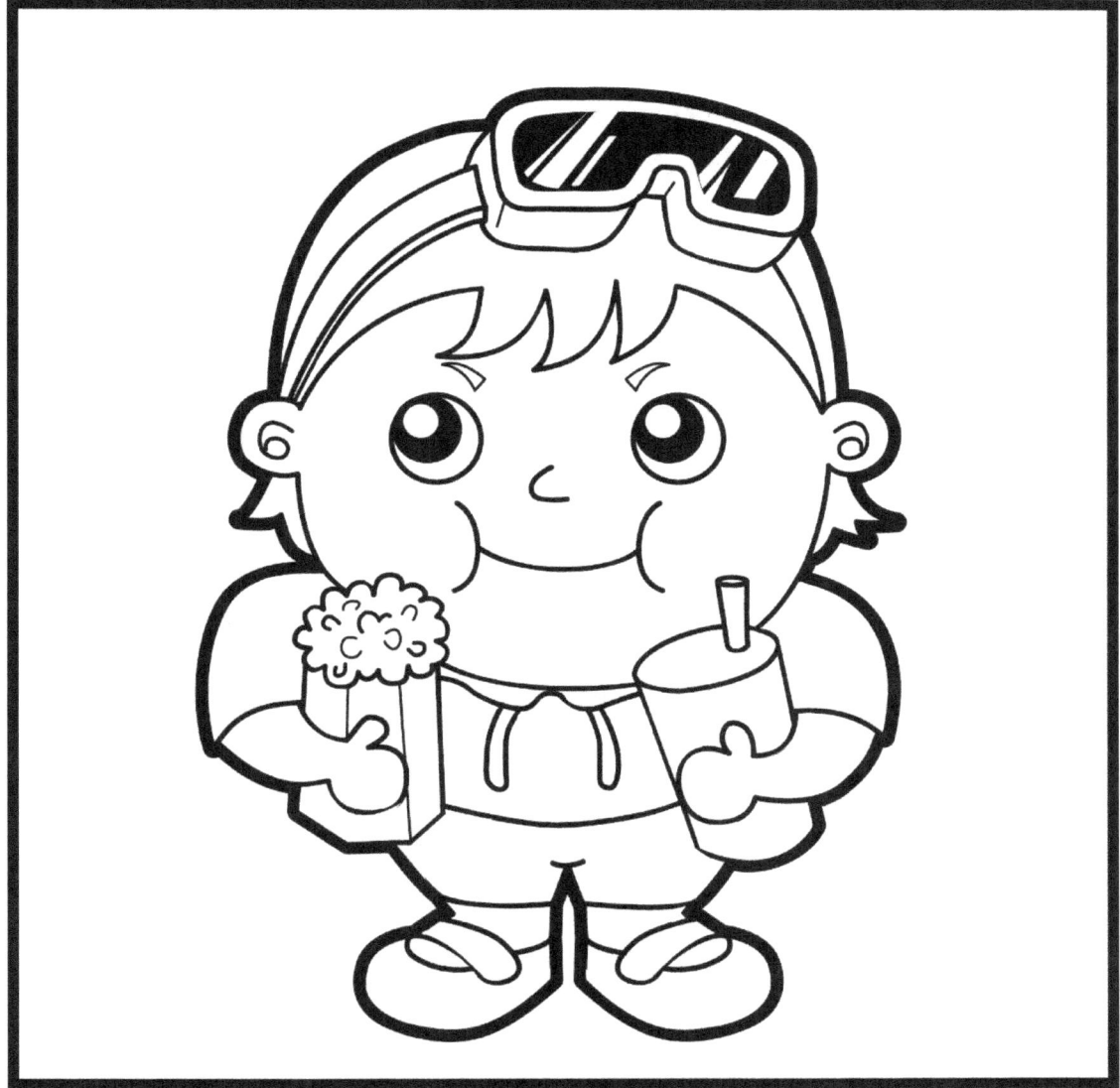

note:

_____

_____

_____

JUNE 20TH

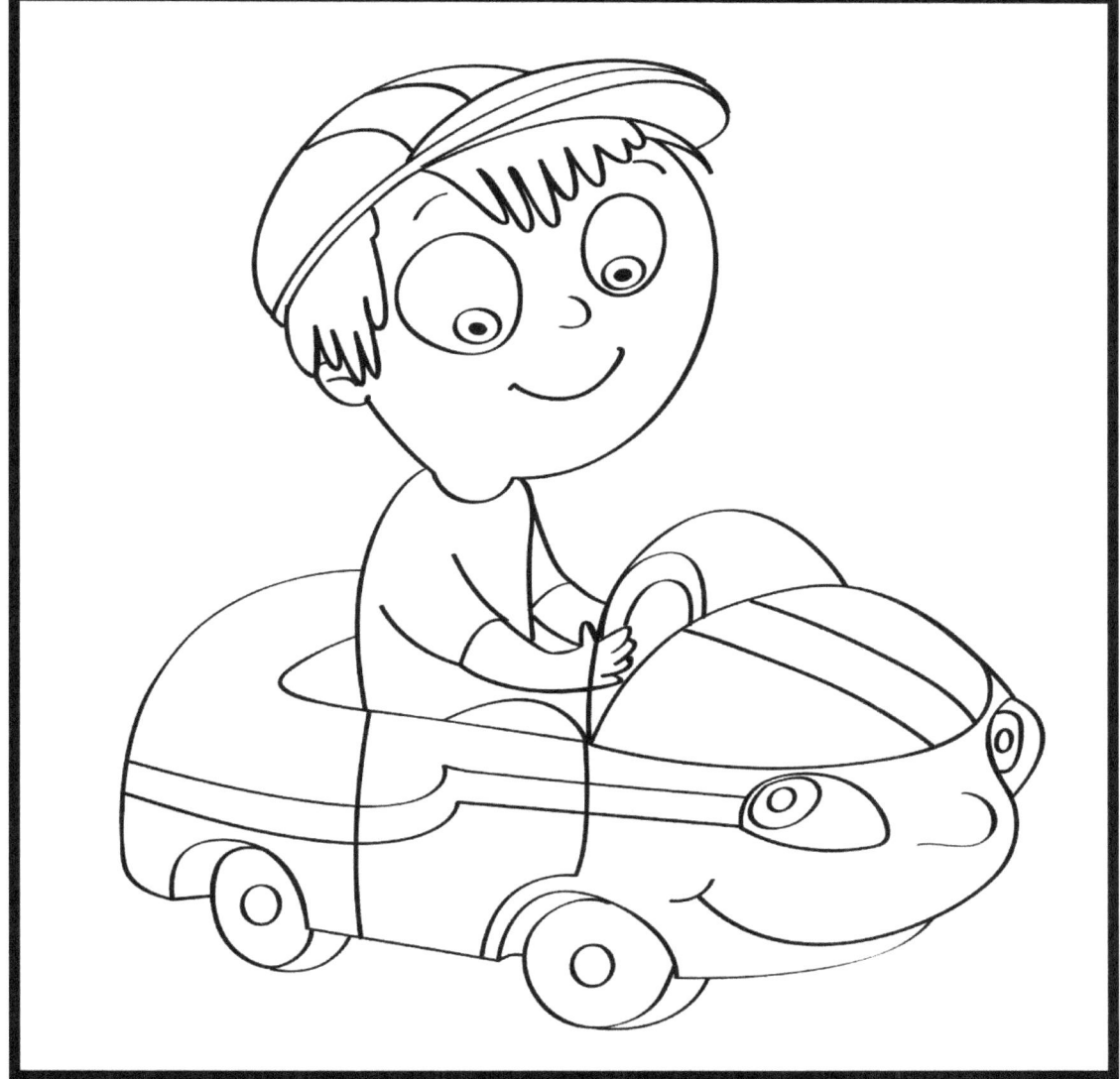

note:

_____

_____

_____

JUNE 21TH

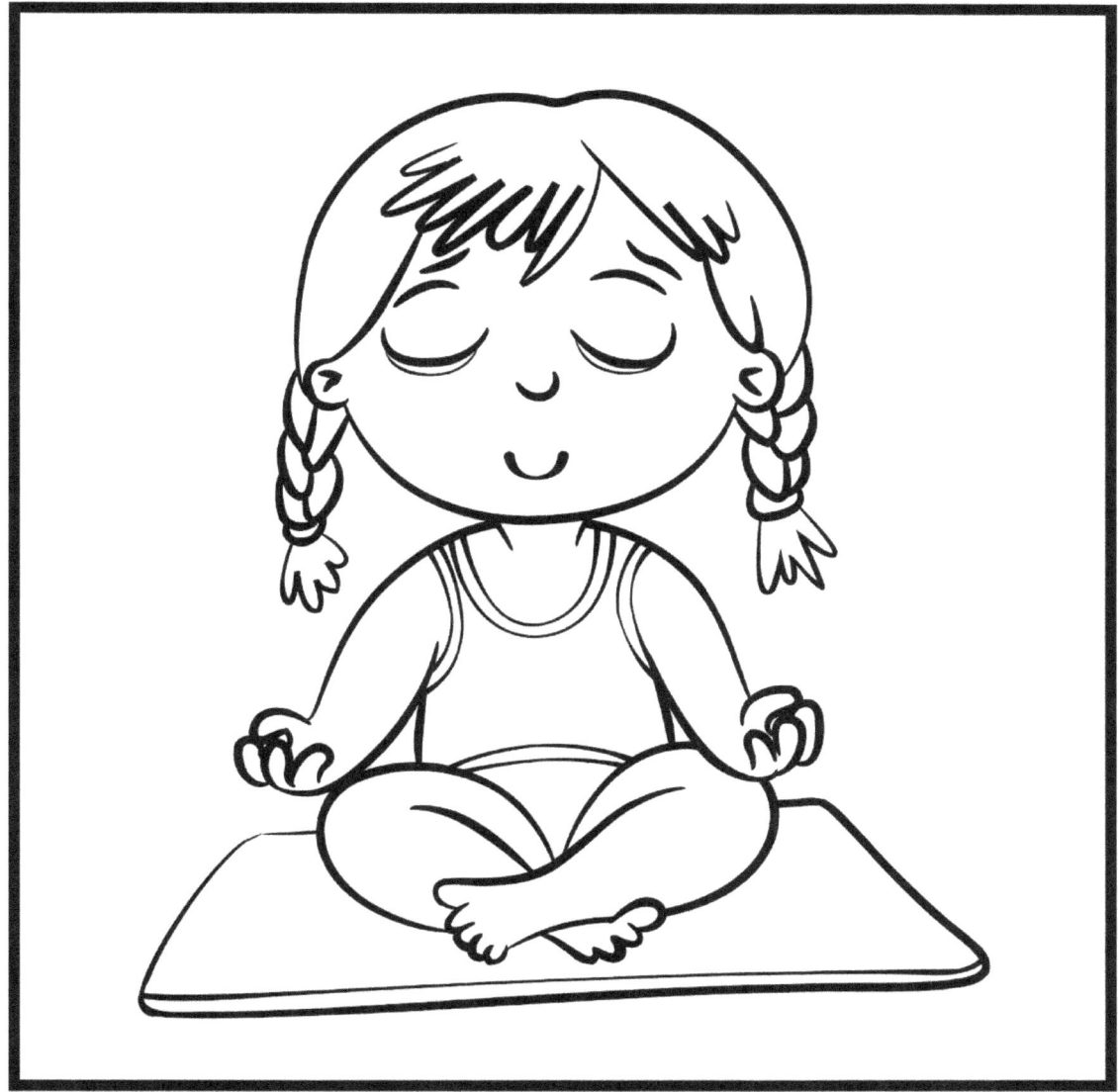

note:

_____

_____

_____

JUNE 22TH

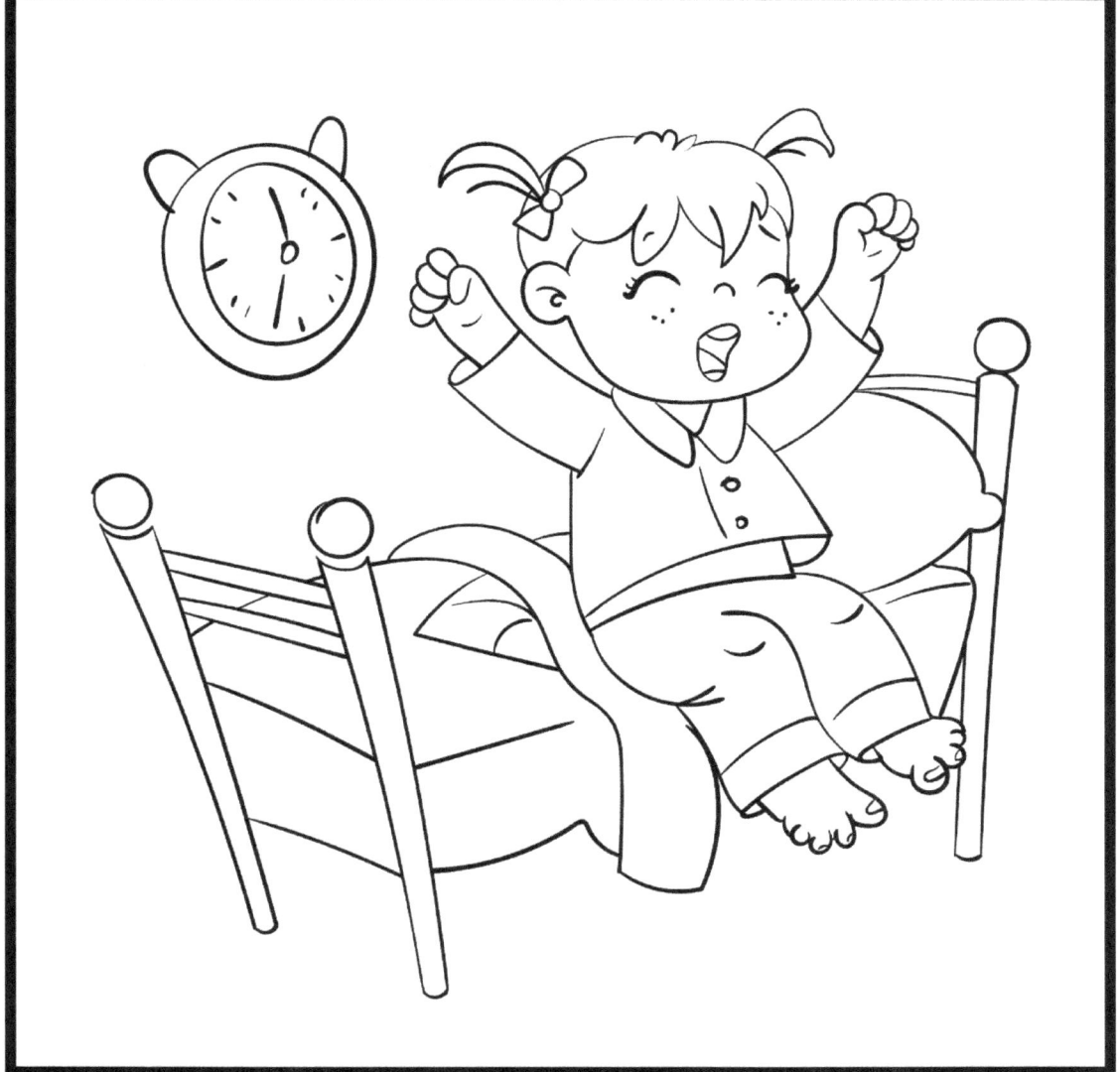

note:

_____

_____

_____

JUNE 23TH

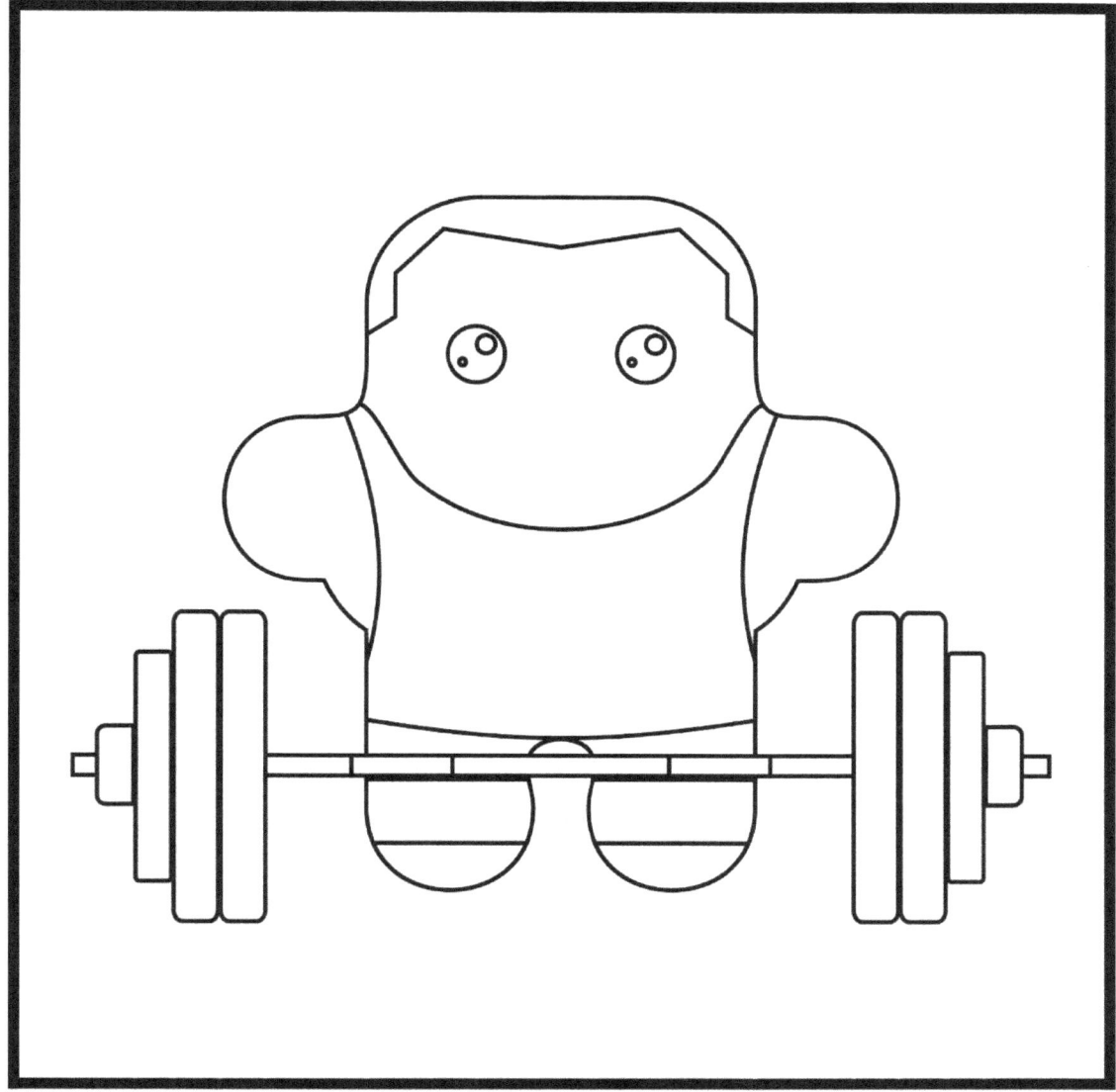

note:

_____

_____

_____

JUNE 24TH

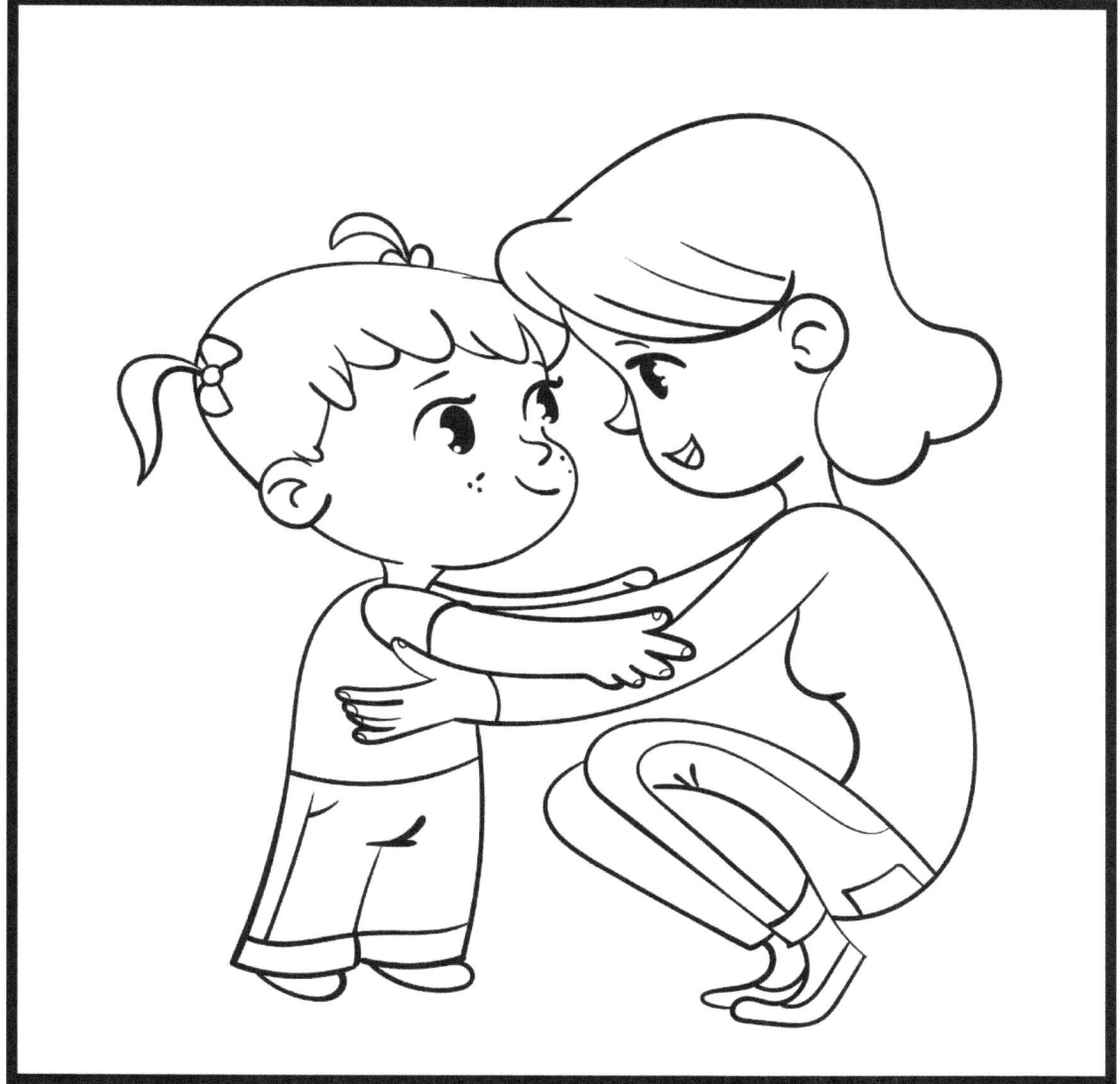

note:

_____

_____

_____

JUNE 25TH

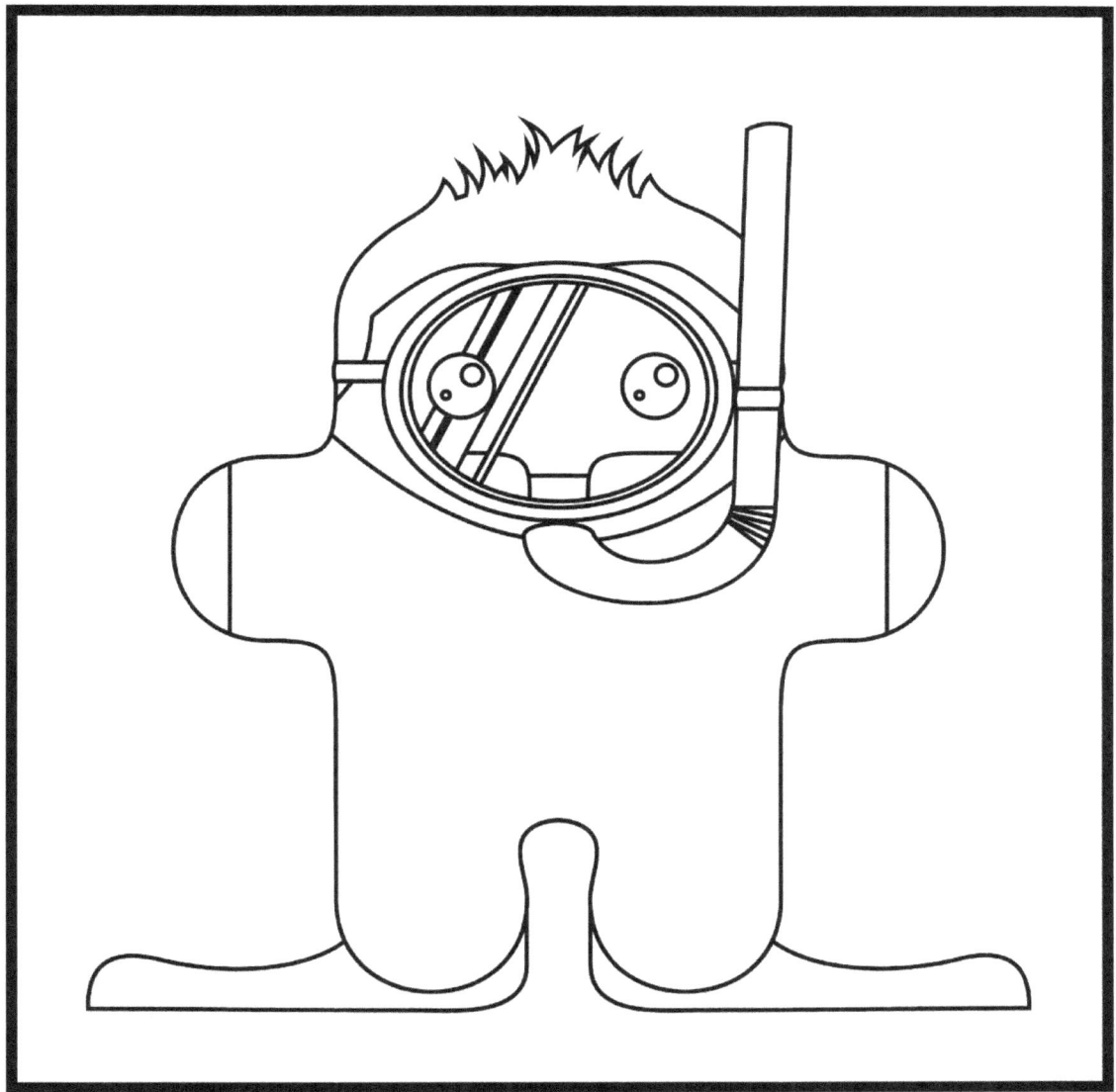

note:

_____

_____

_____

JUNE 26TH

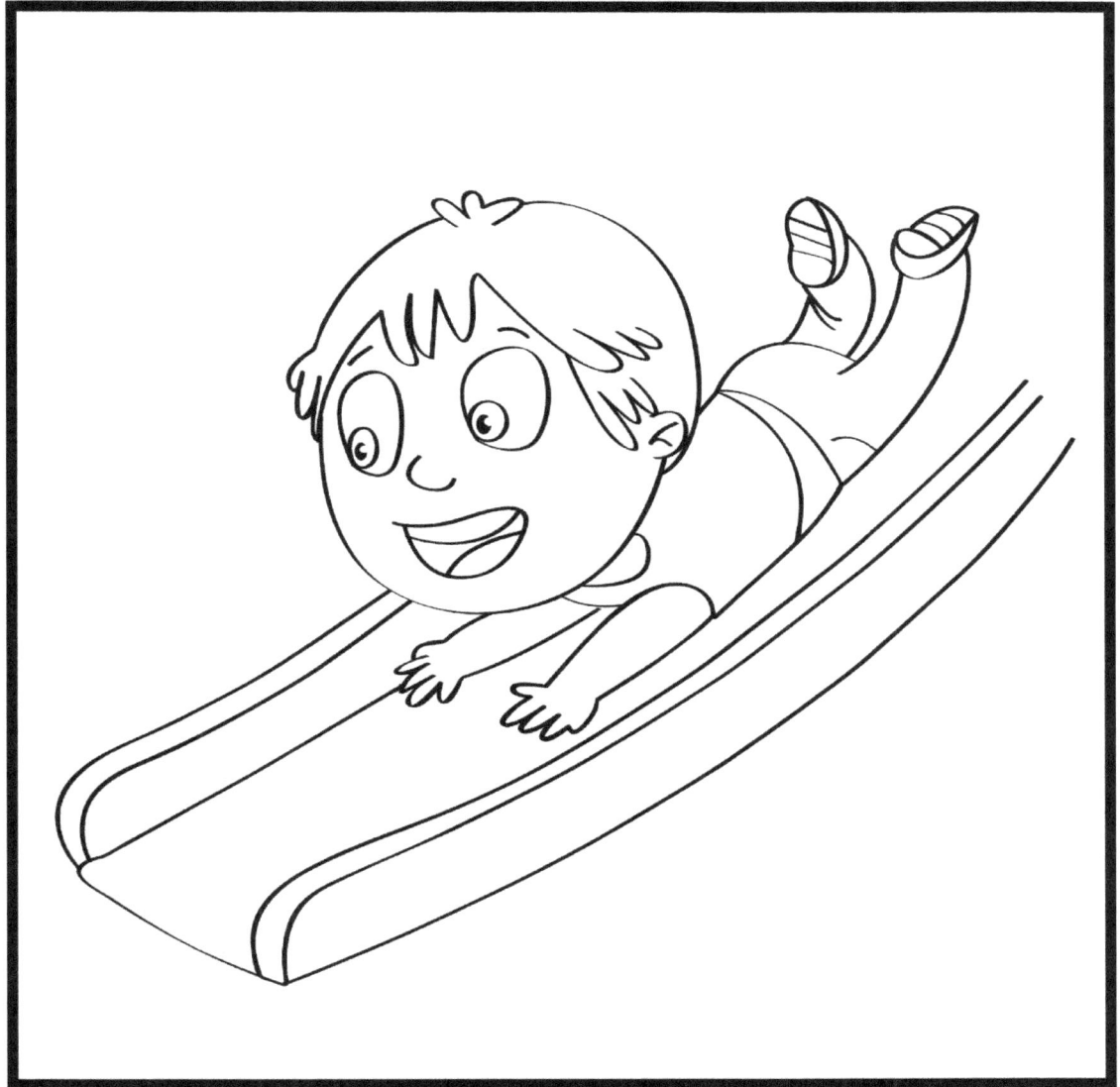

note:

_____

_____

_____

JUNE 27TH

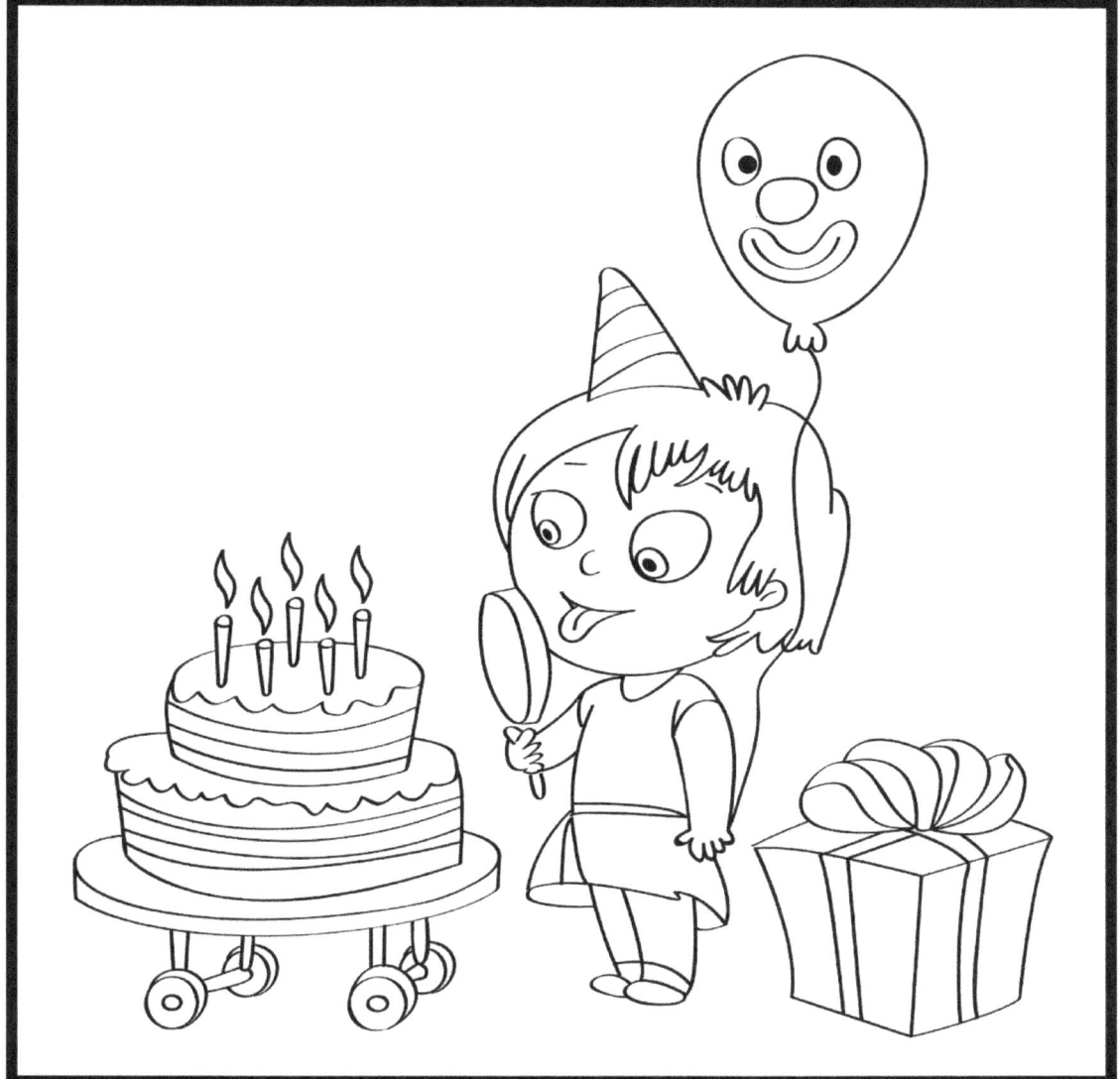

note:

_____

_____

_____

JUNE 28TH

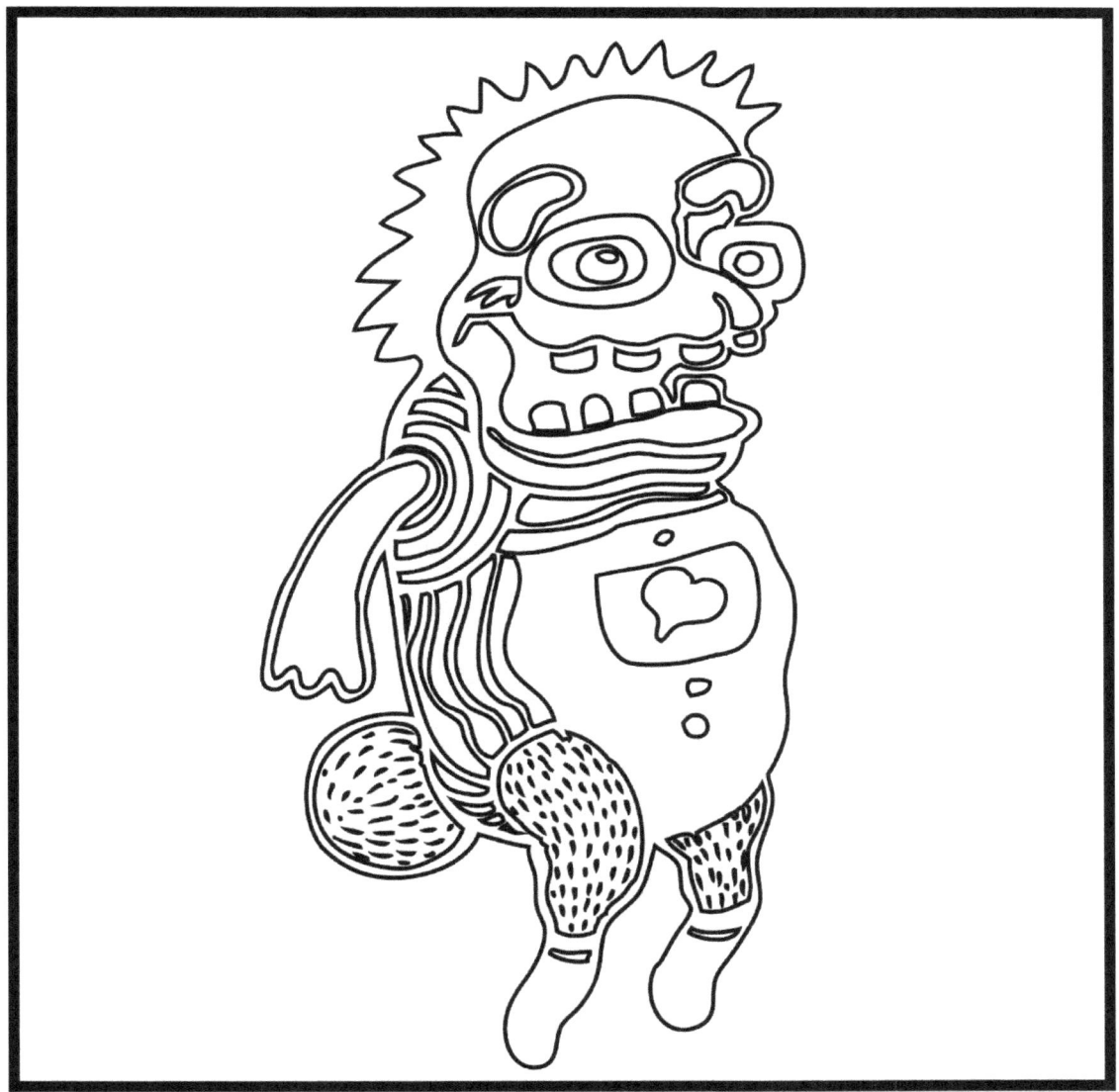

note:

_____

_____

_____

JUNE 29TH

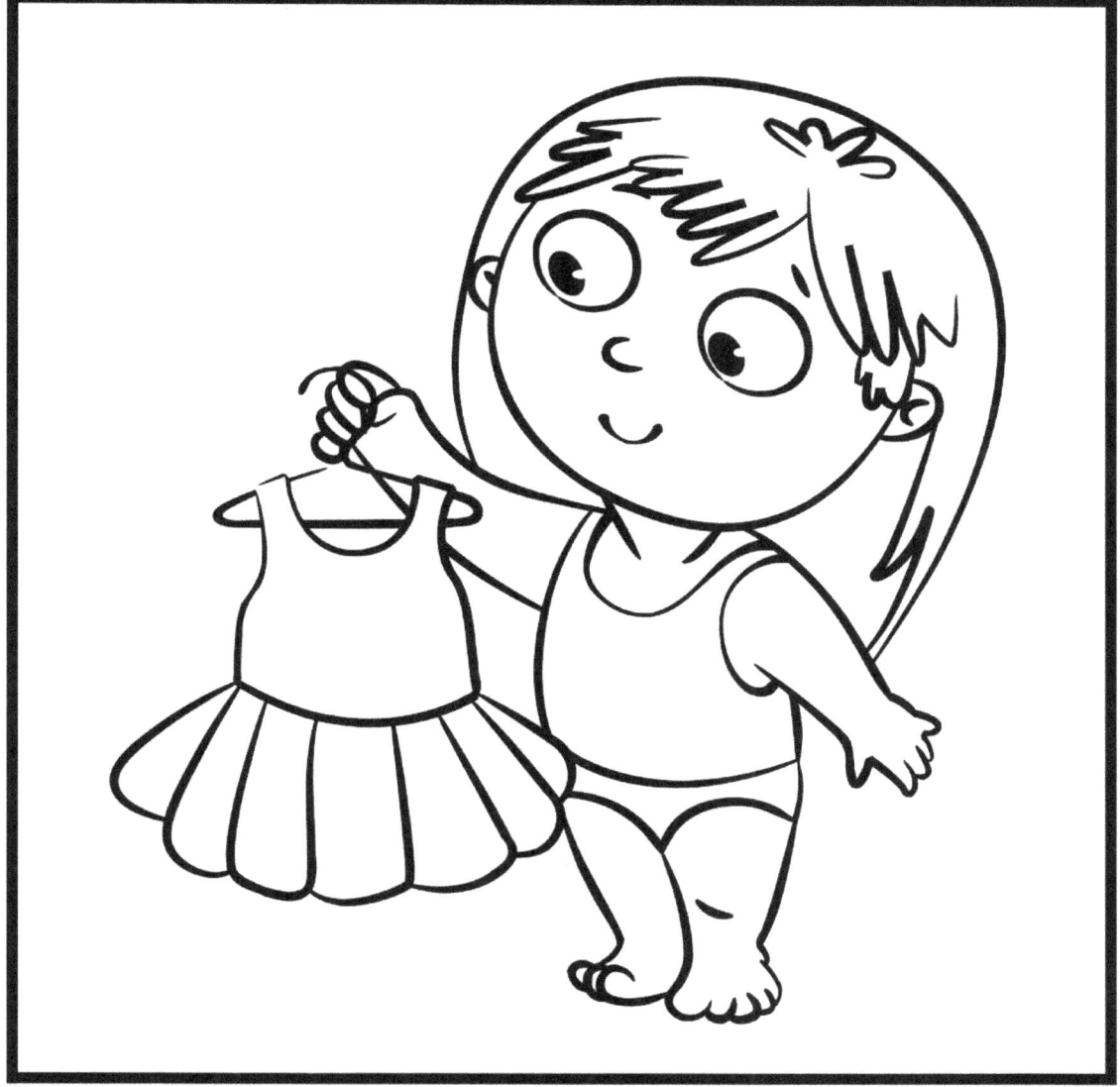

note:

_____

_____

_____

JUNE 30TH

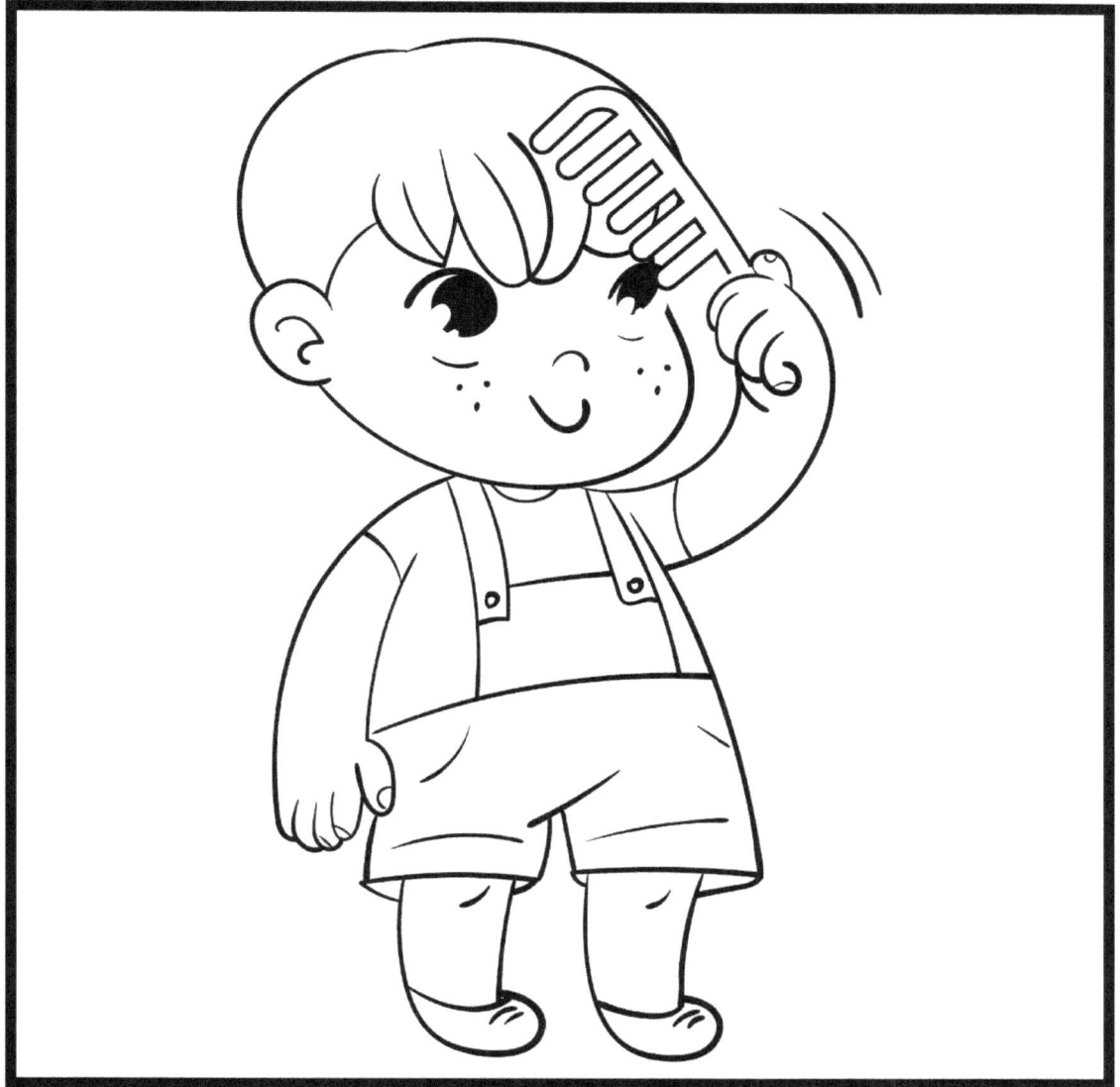

note:

_____

_____

_____

JUNE 31TH

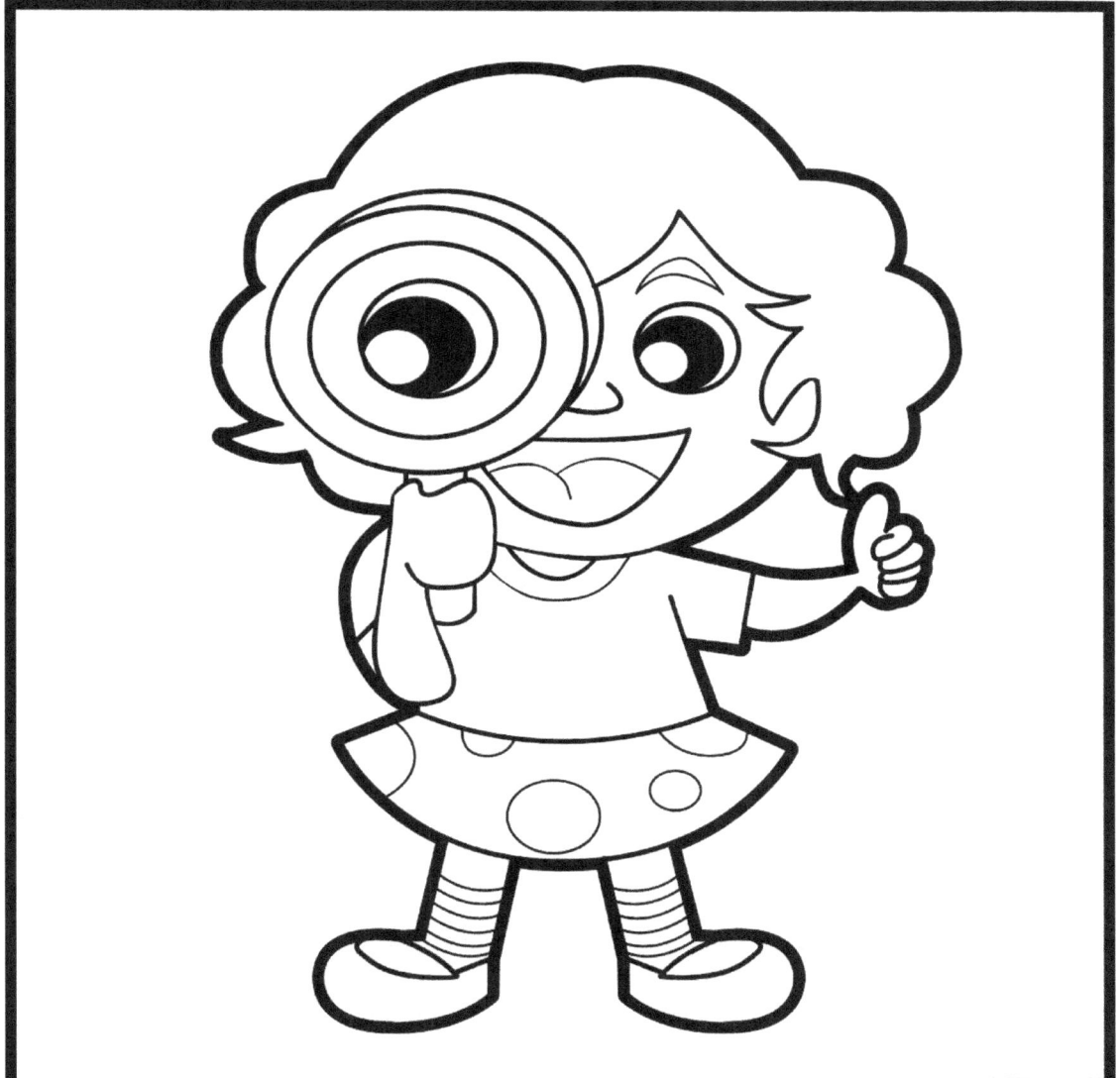

note:

_____

_____

_____

JUNE 32TH

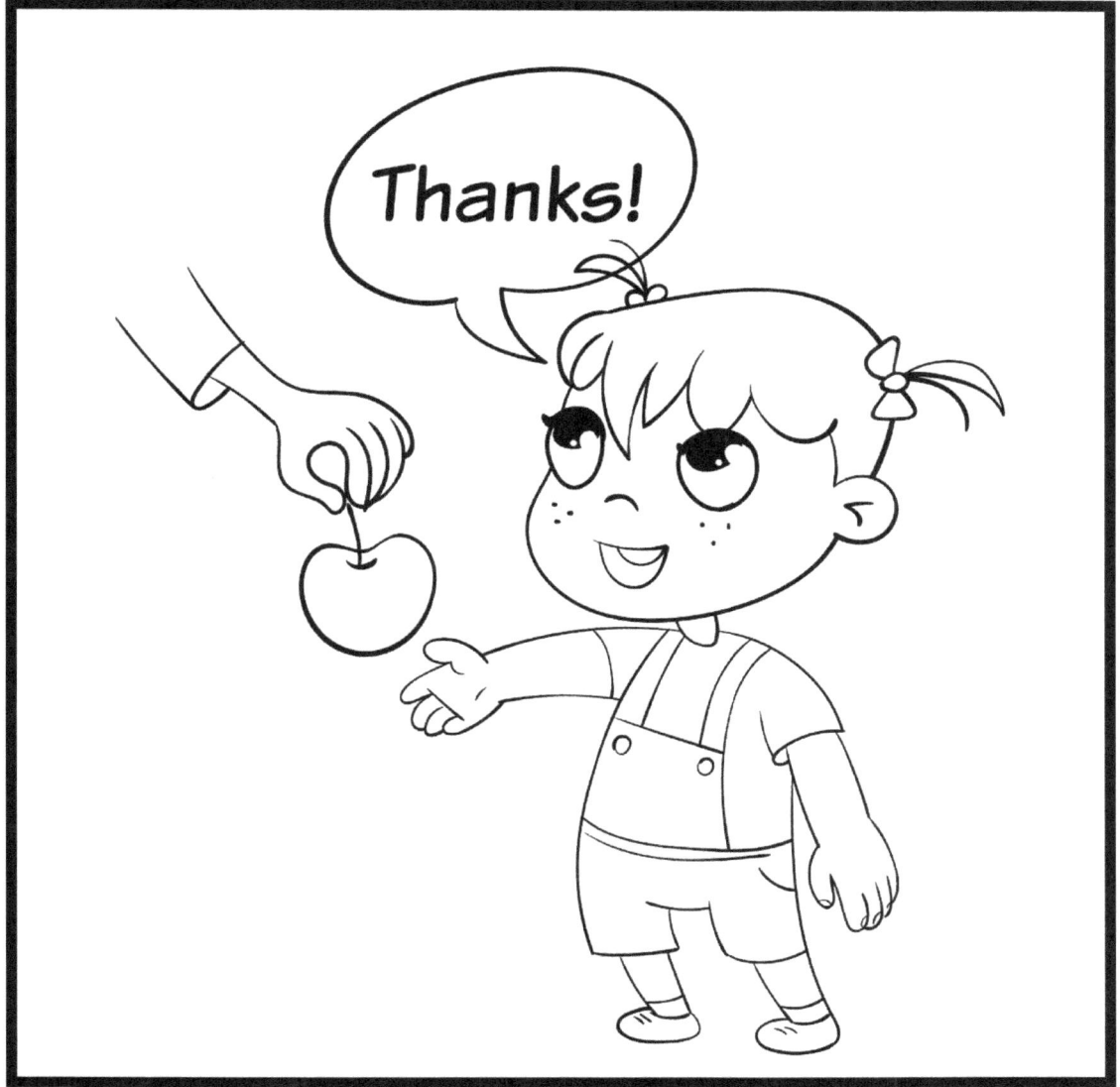

note:

_____

_____

_____

JUNE 33TH

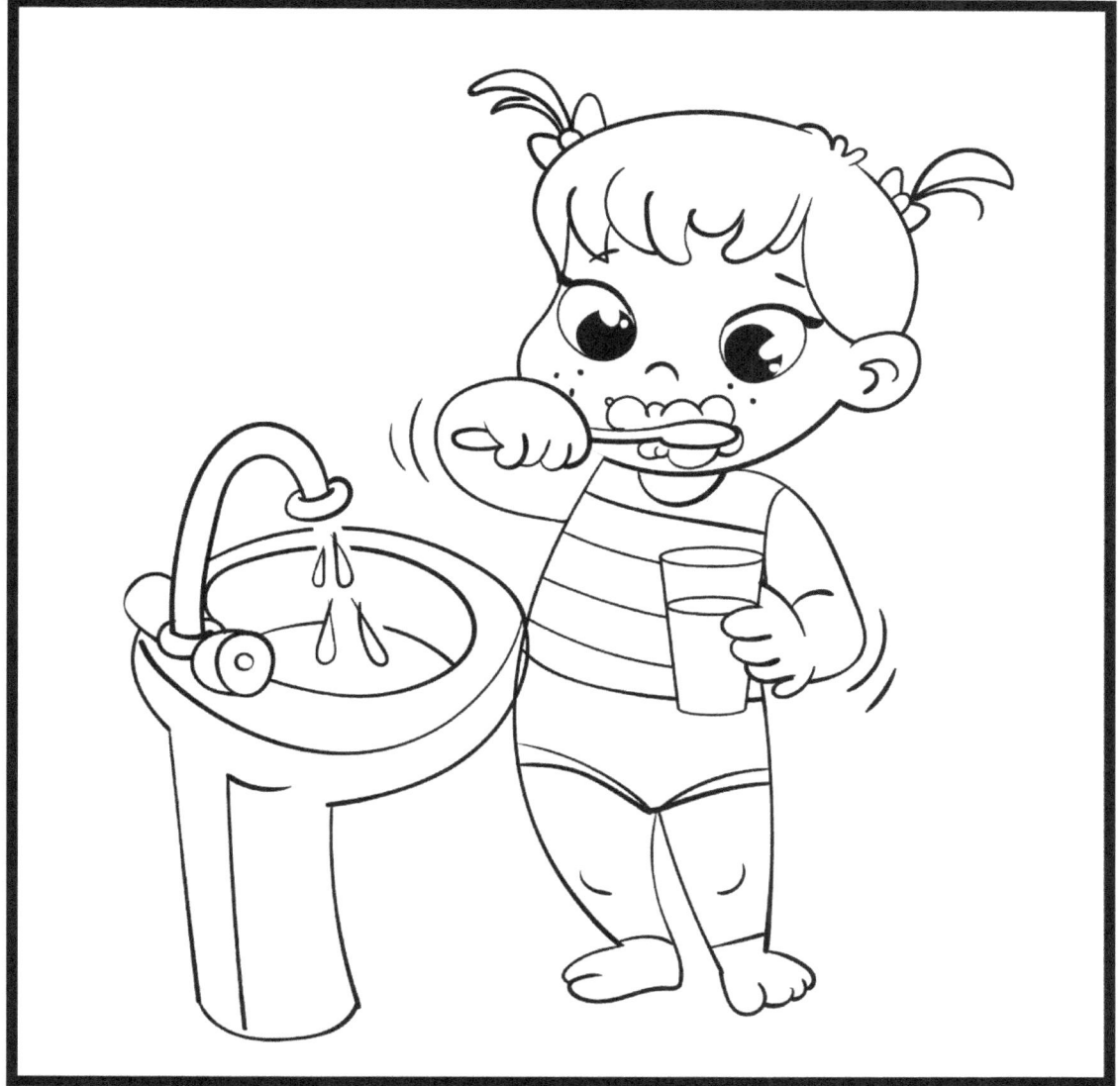

note:

_____

_____

_____

JUNE 34TH

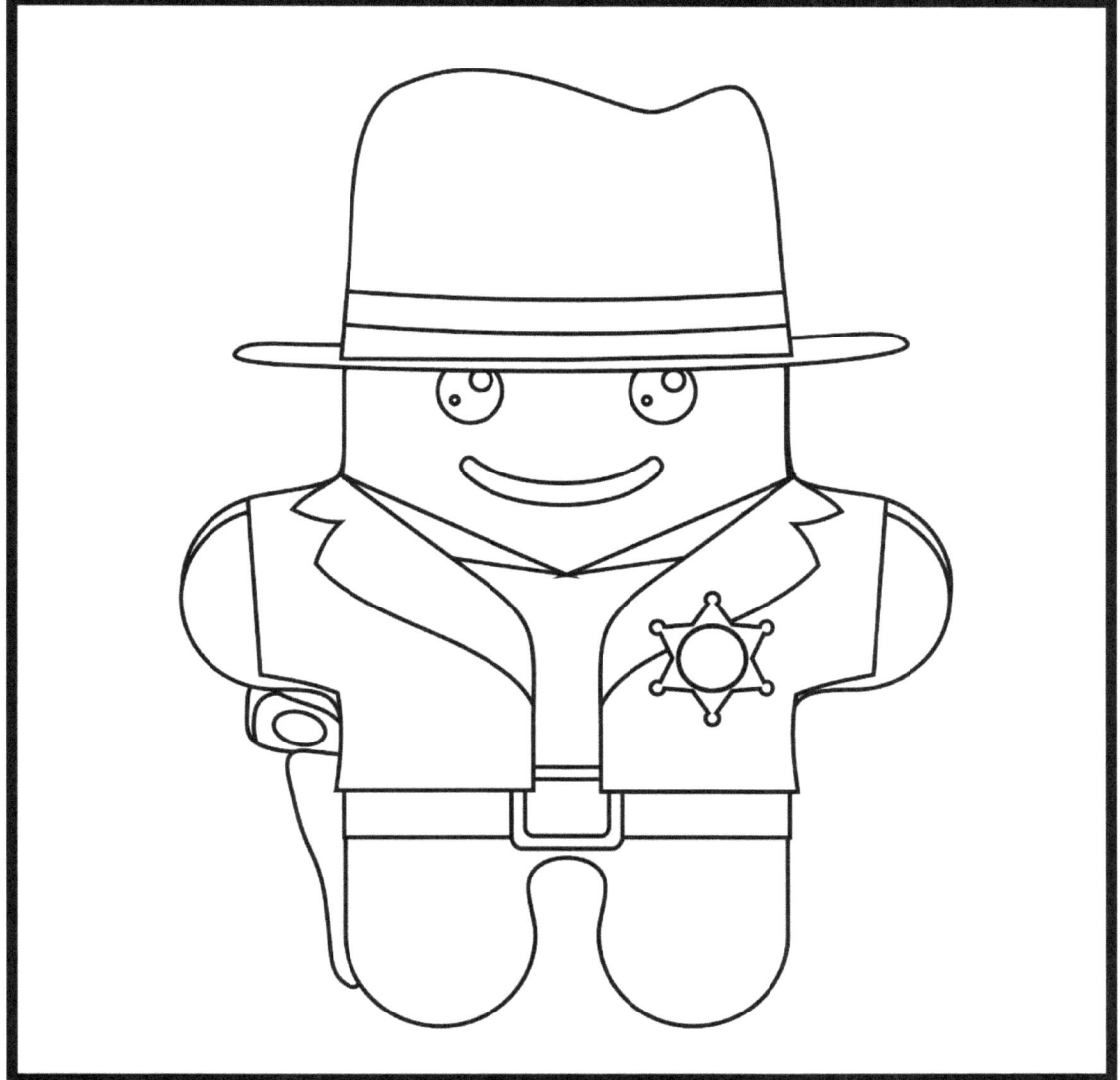

note:

_____

_____

_____

JUNE 35TH

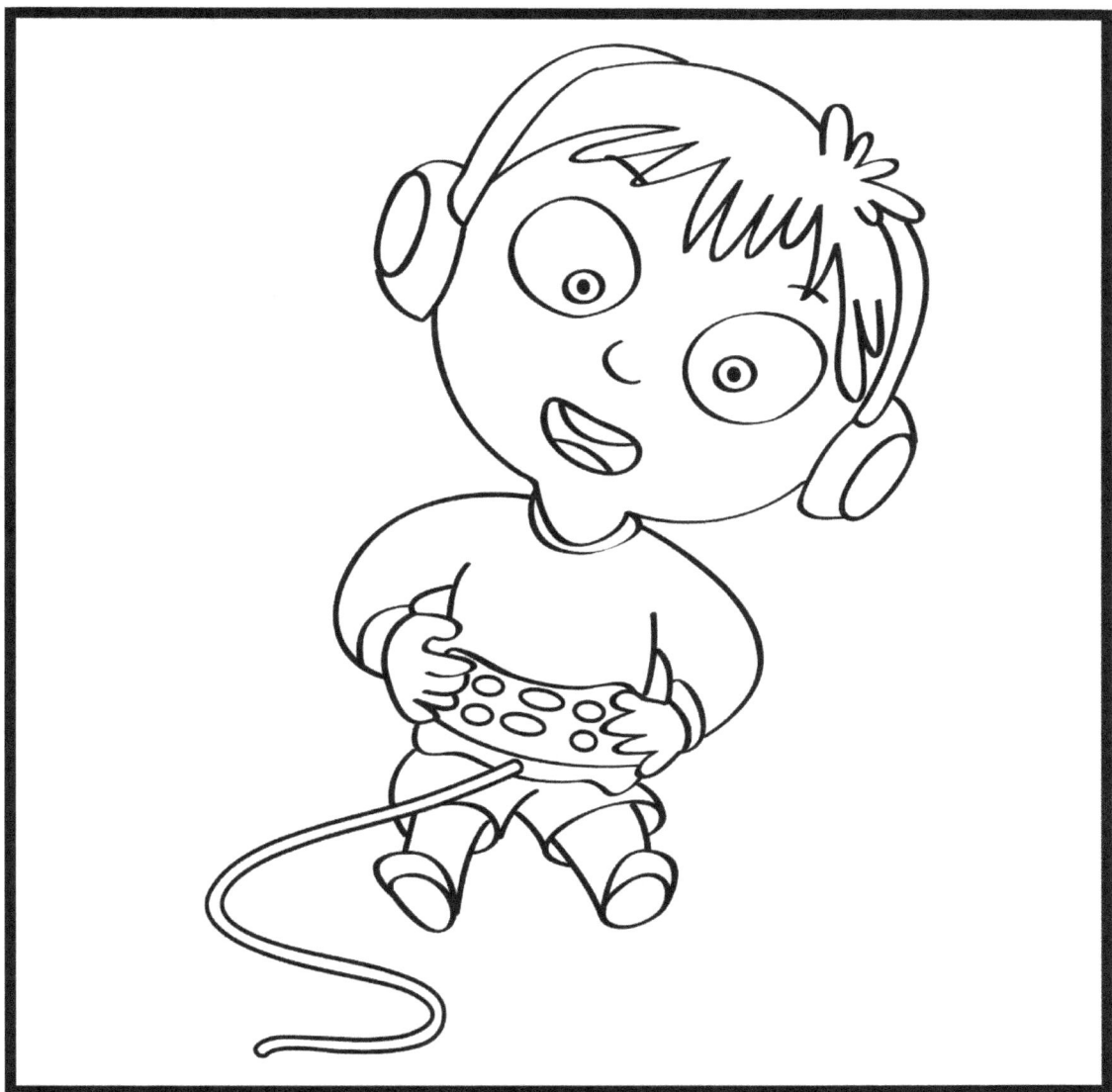

note:

_____

_____

_____

JUNE 36TH

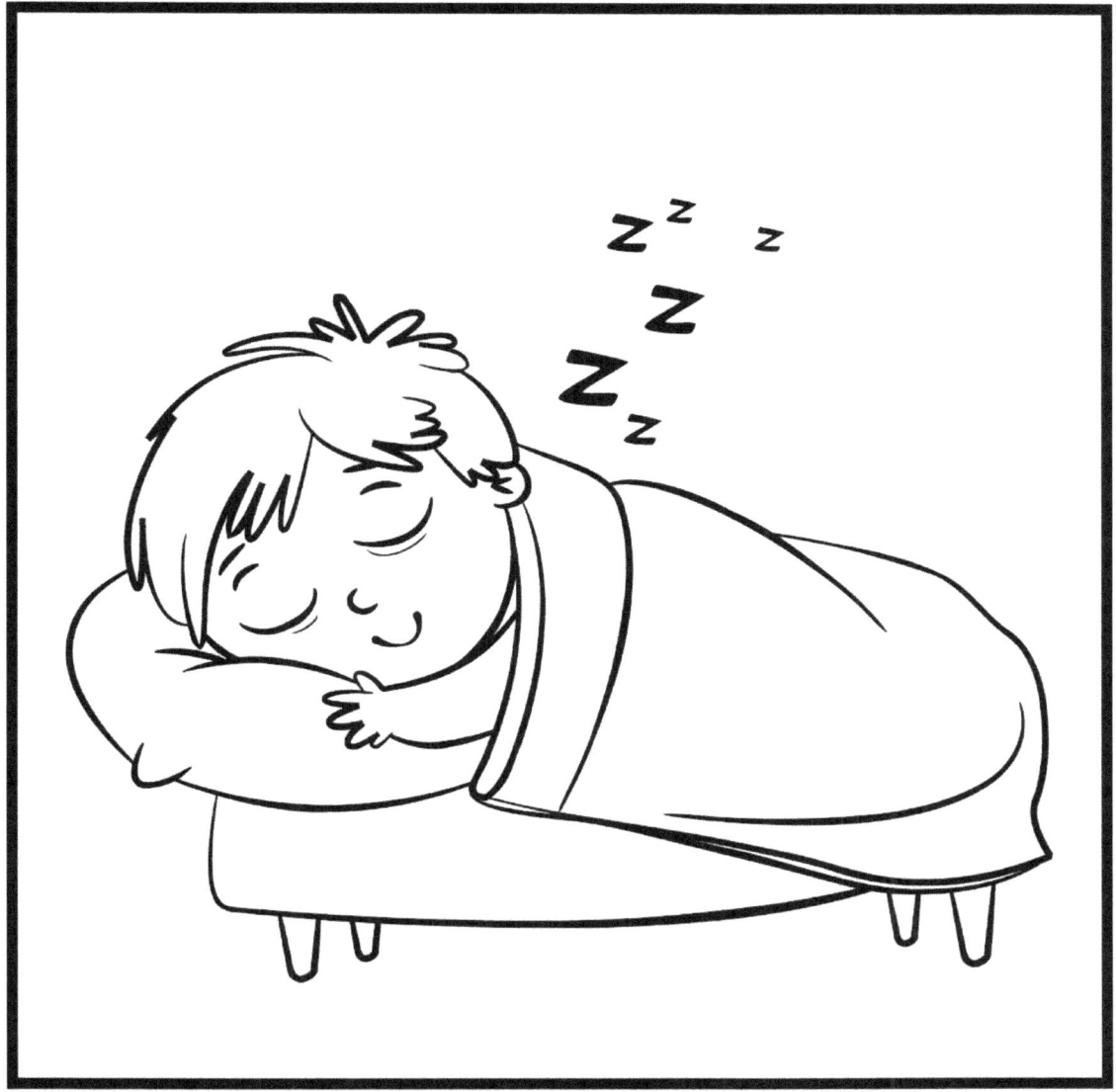

note:

_____

_____

_____

JUNE 37TH

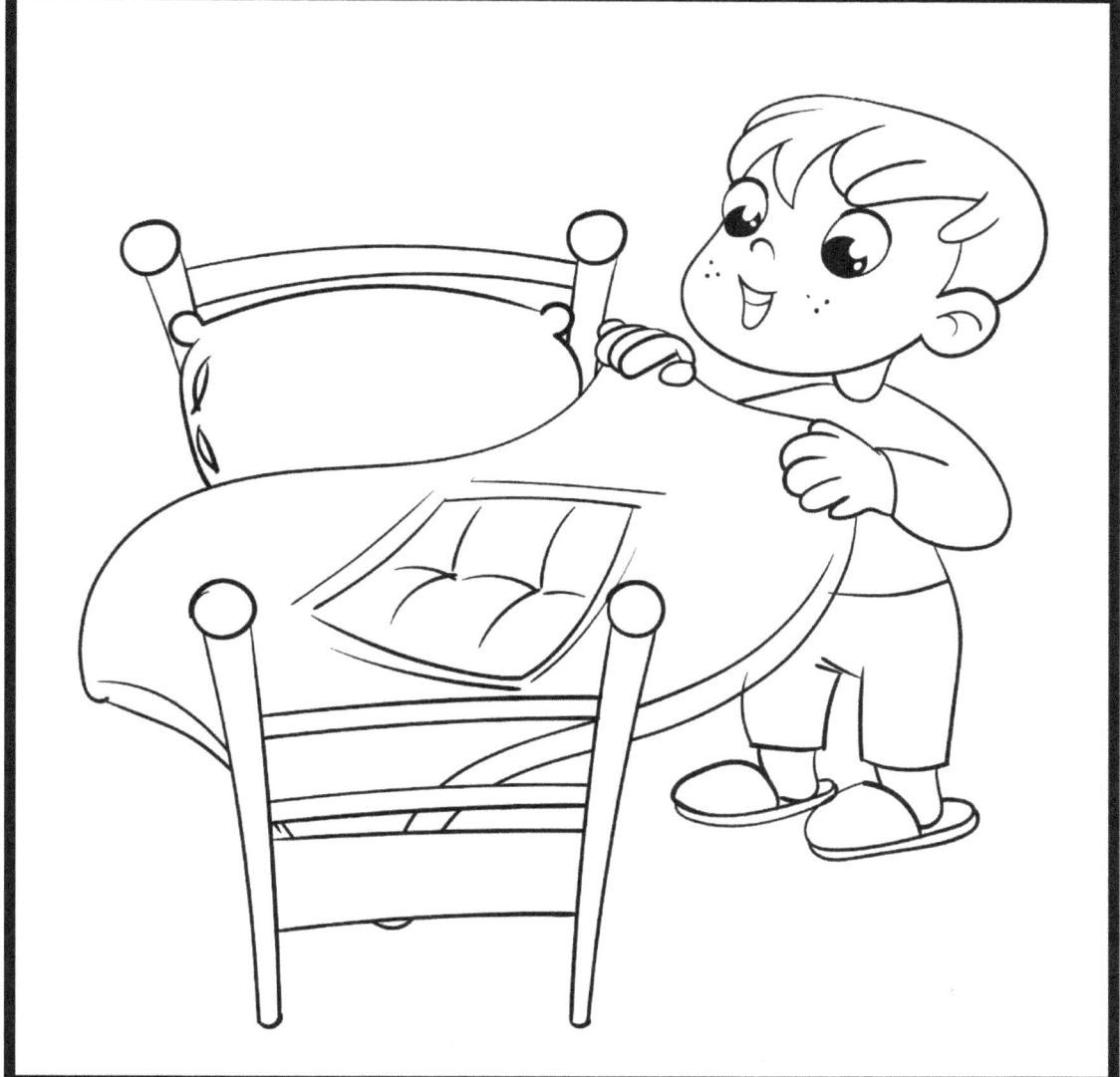

note:

_____

_____

_____

JUNE 38TH

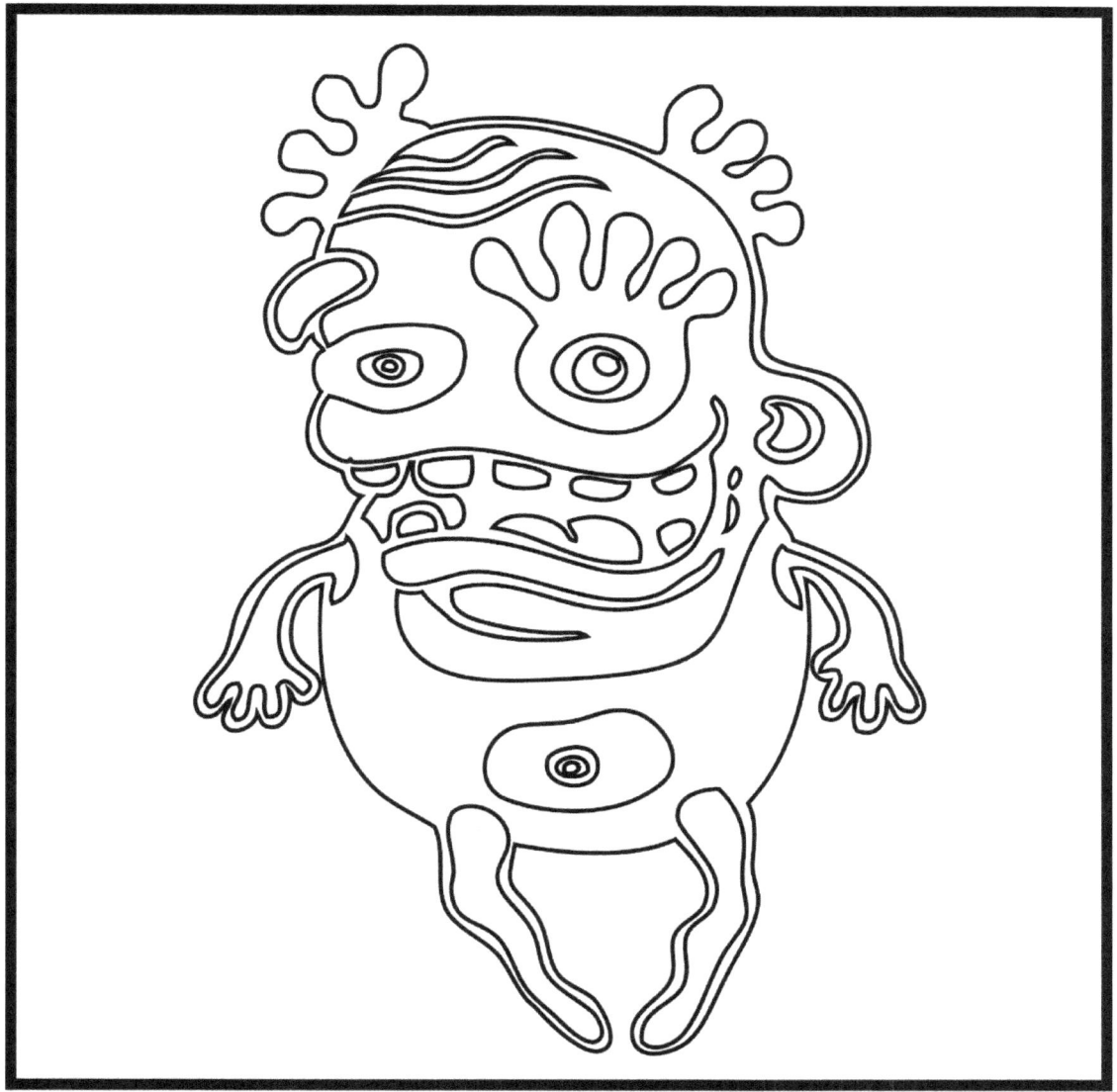

note:

_____

_____

_____

JUNE 39TH

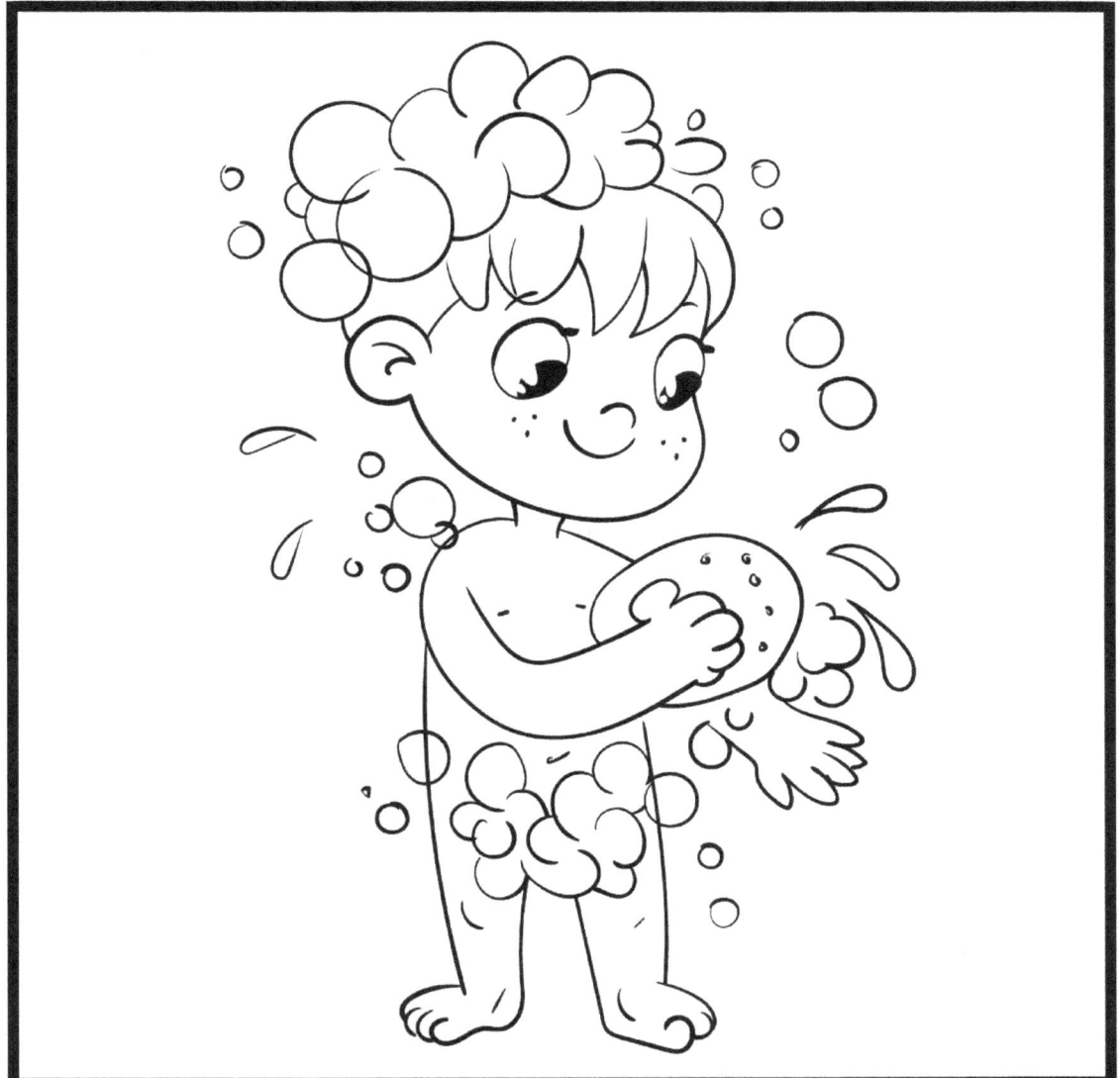

note:

_____

_____

_____

JUNE 40TH

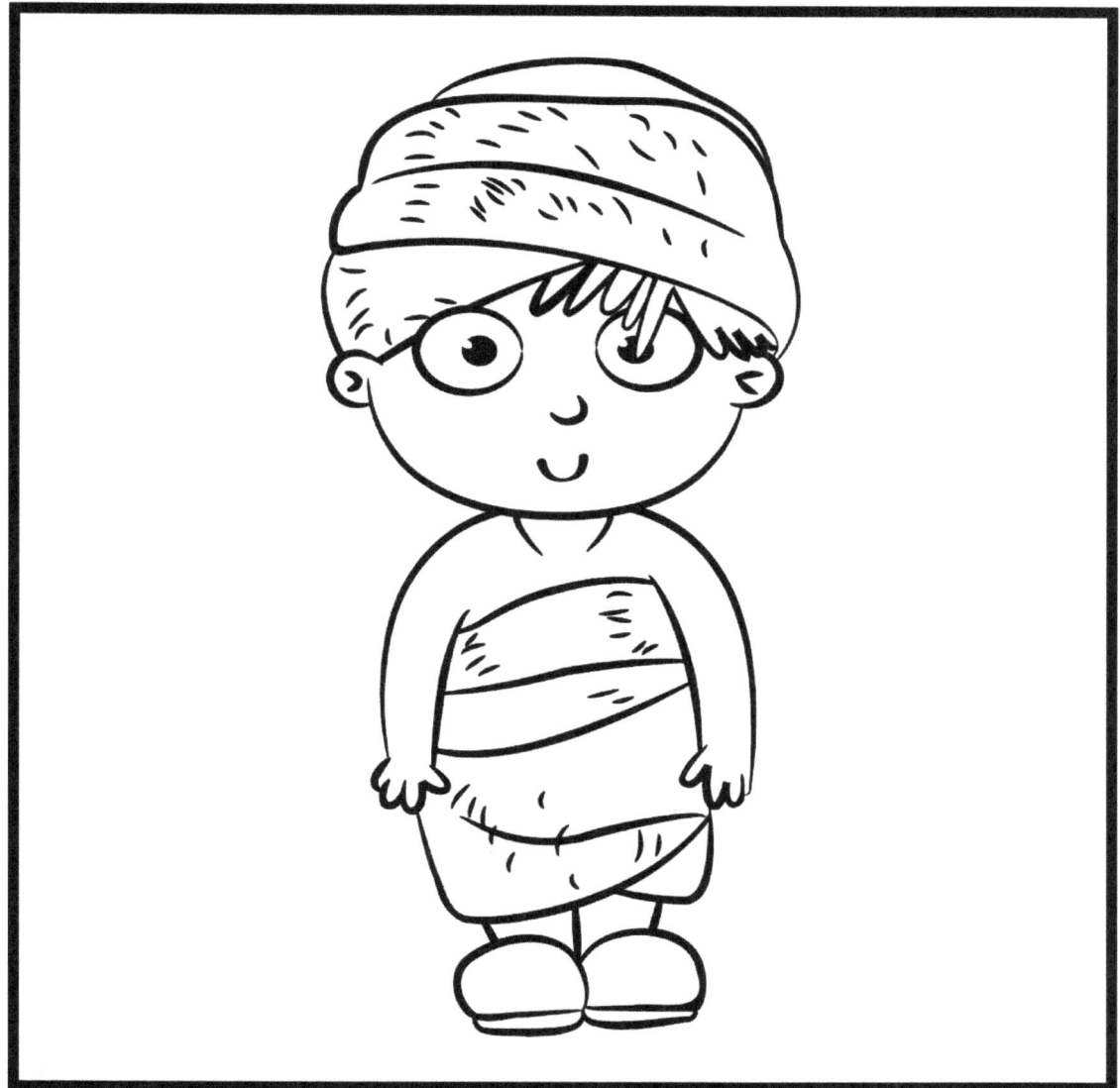

note:

_____

_____

_____

JUNE 41TH

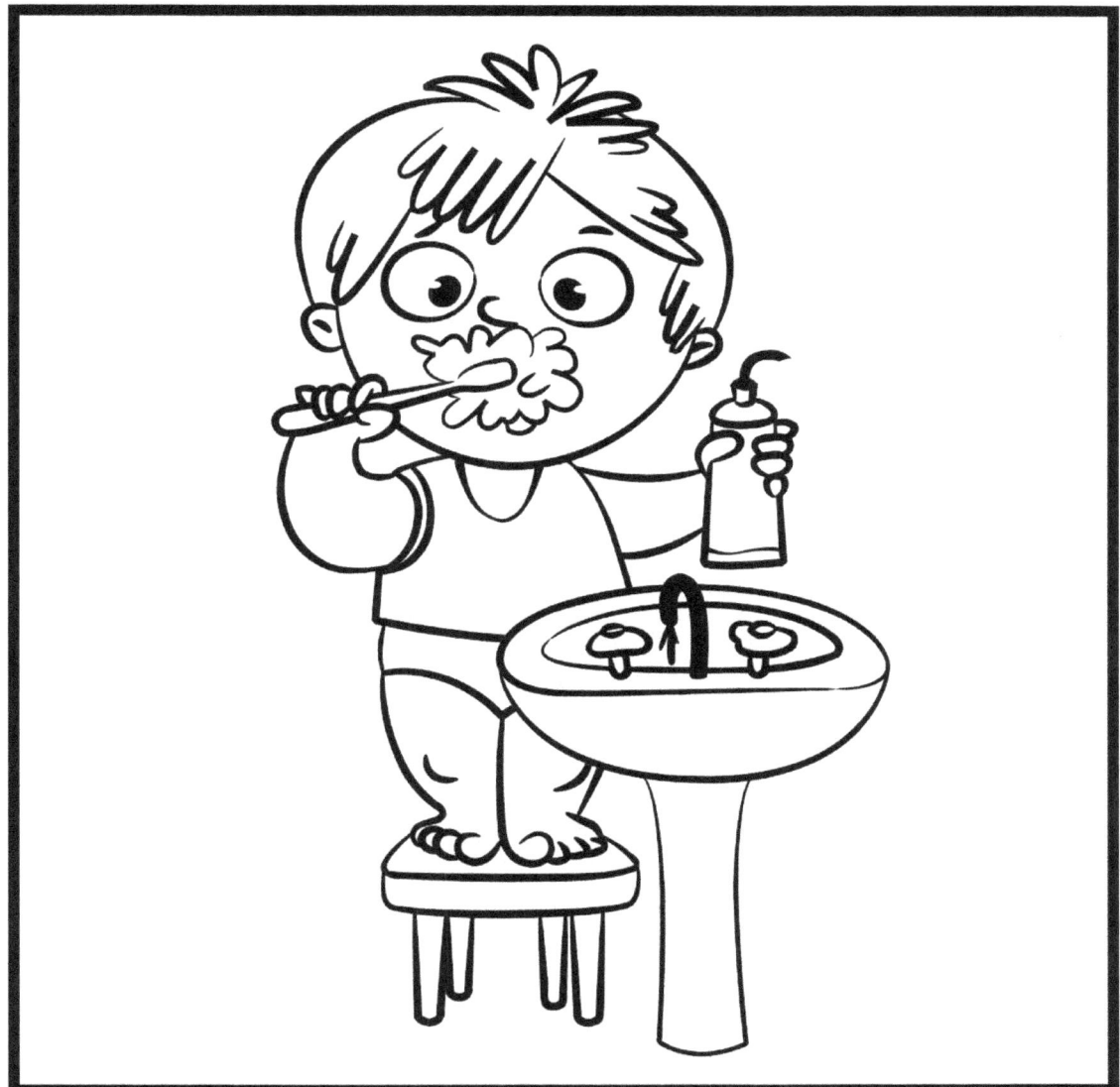

note:

_____

_____

_____

JUNE 42TH

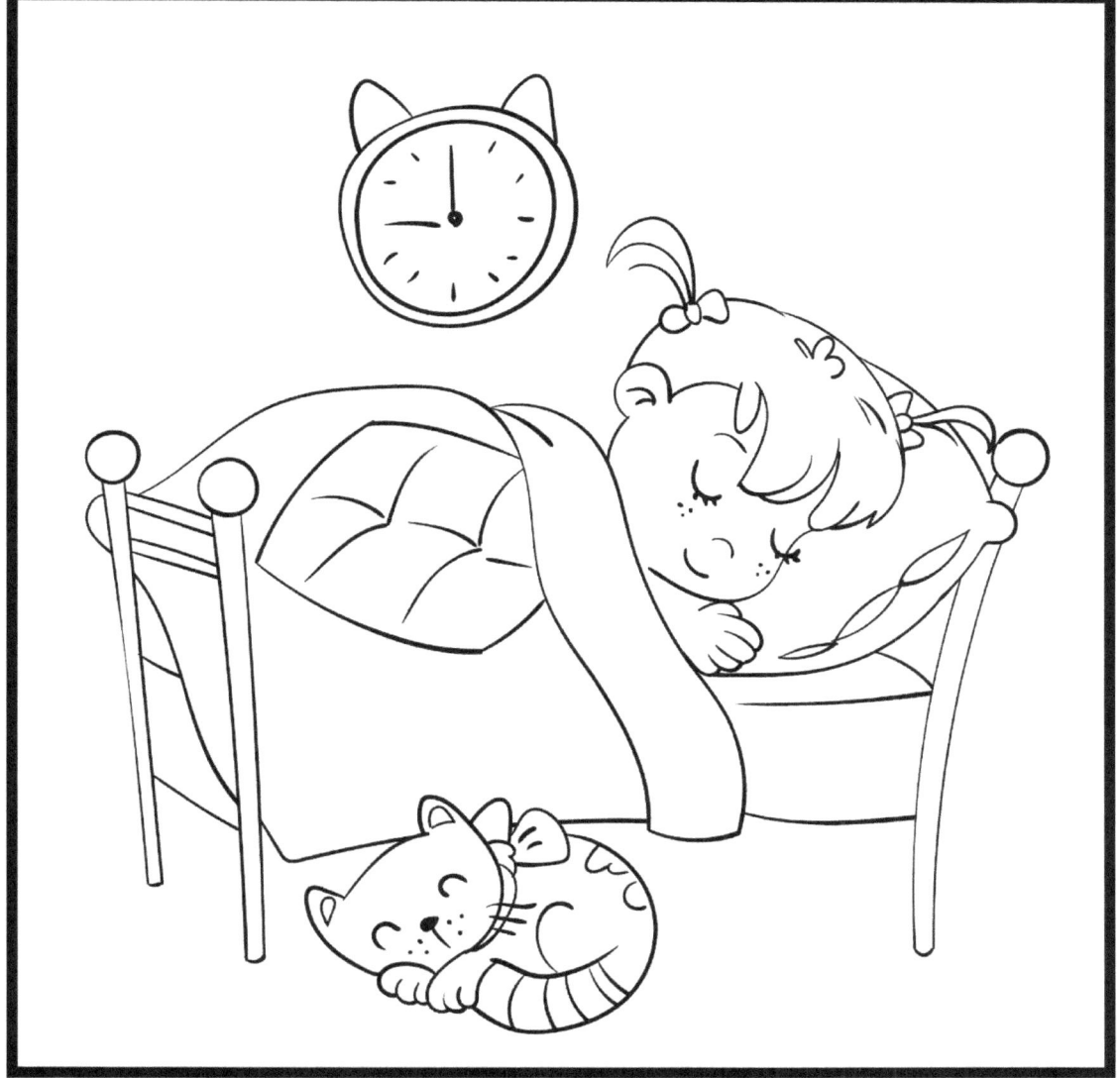

note:

_____

_____

_____

JUNE 43TH

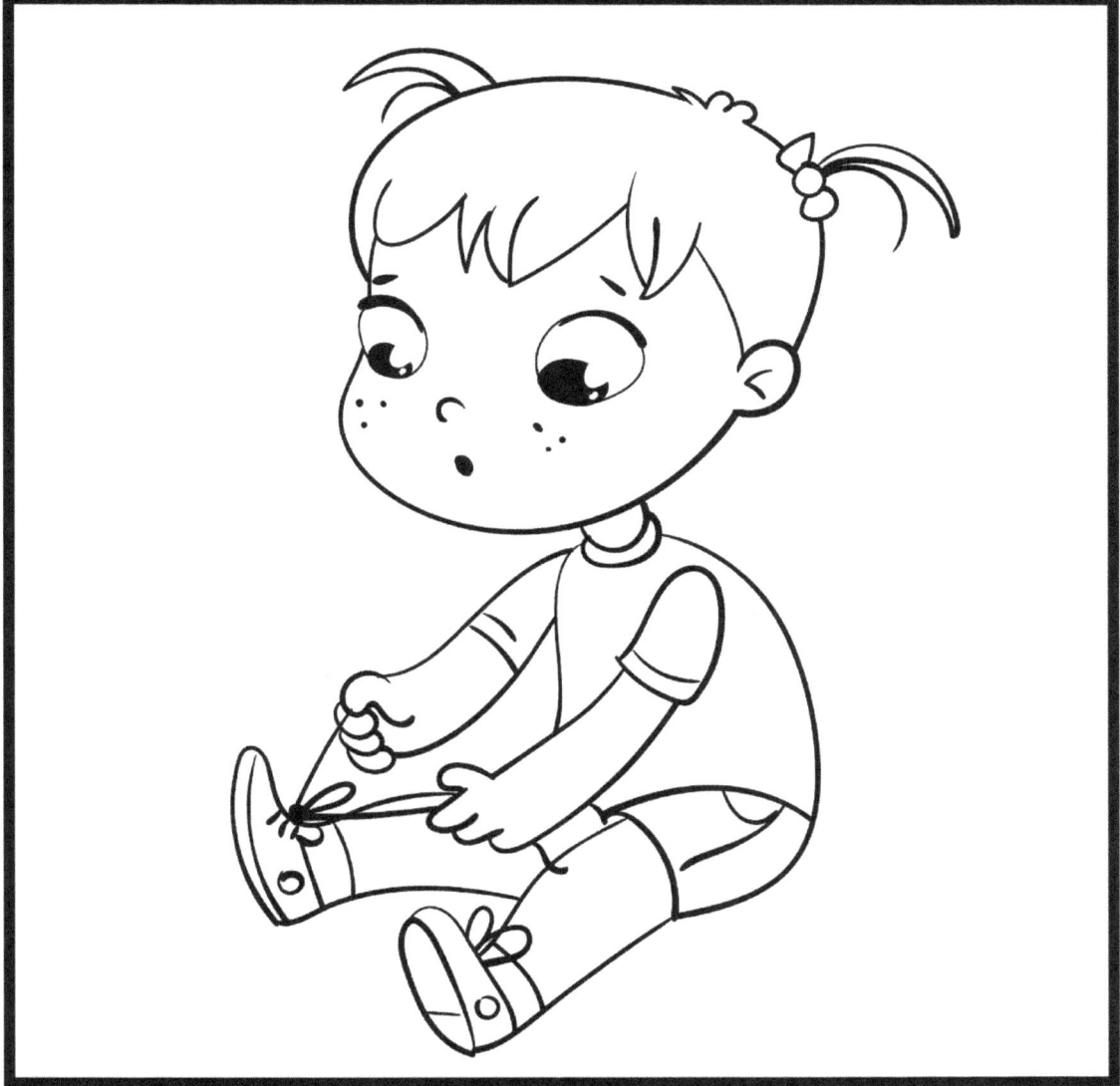

note:

_____

_____

_____

JUNE 44TH

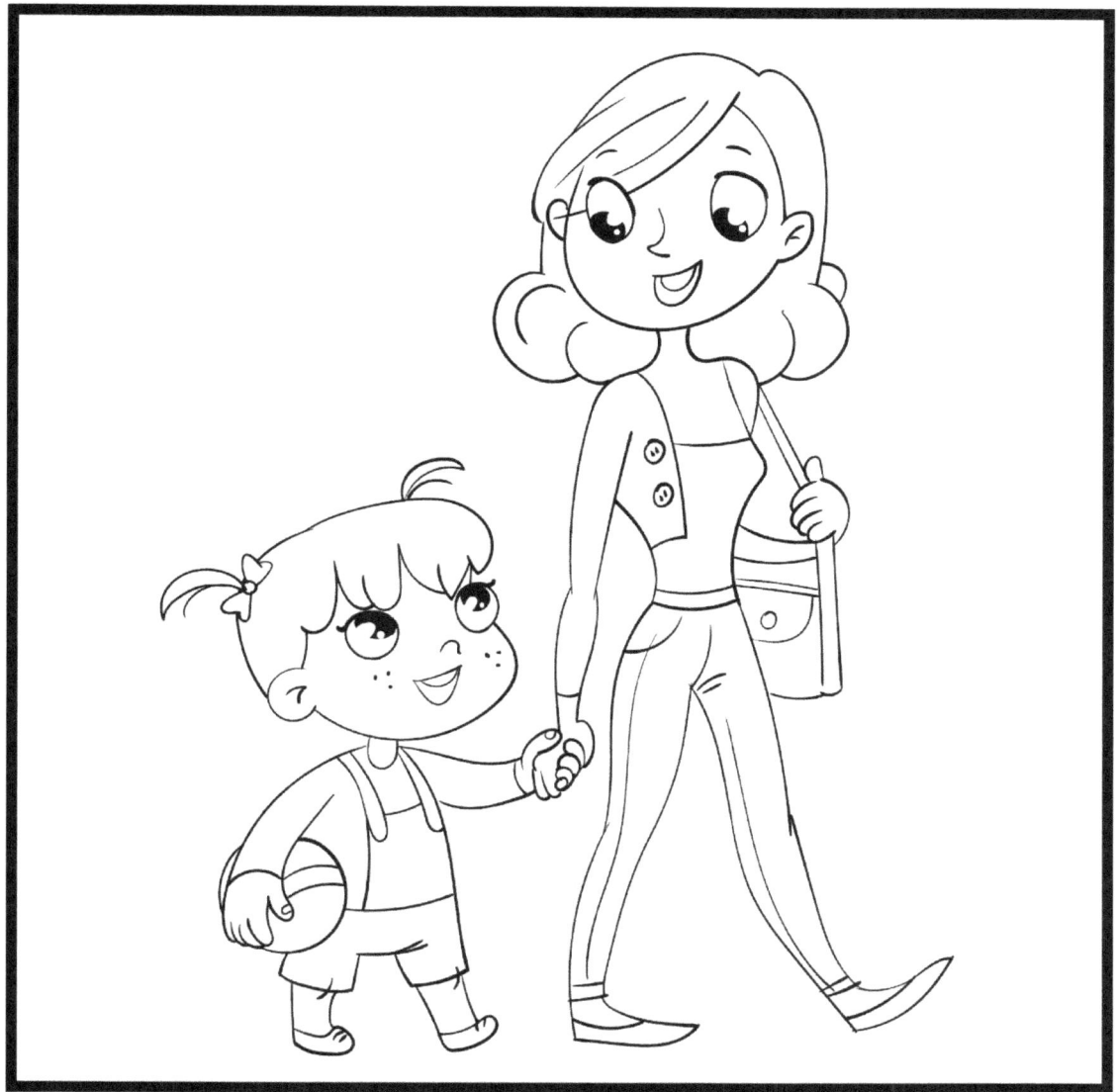

note:

_____

_____

_____

JUNE 45TH

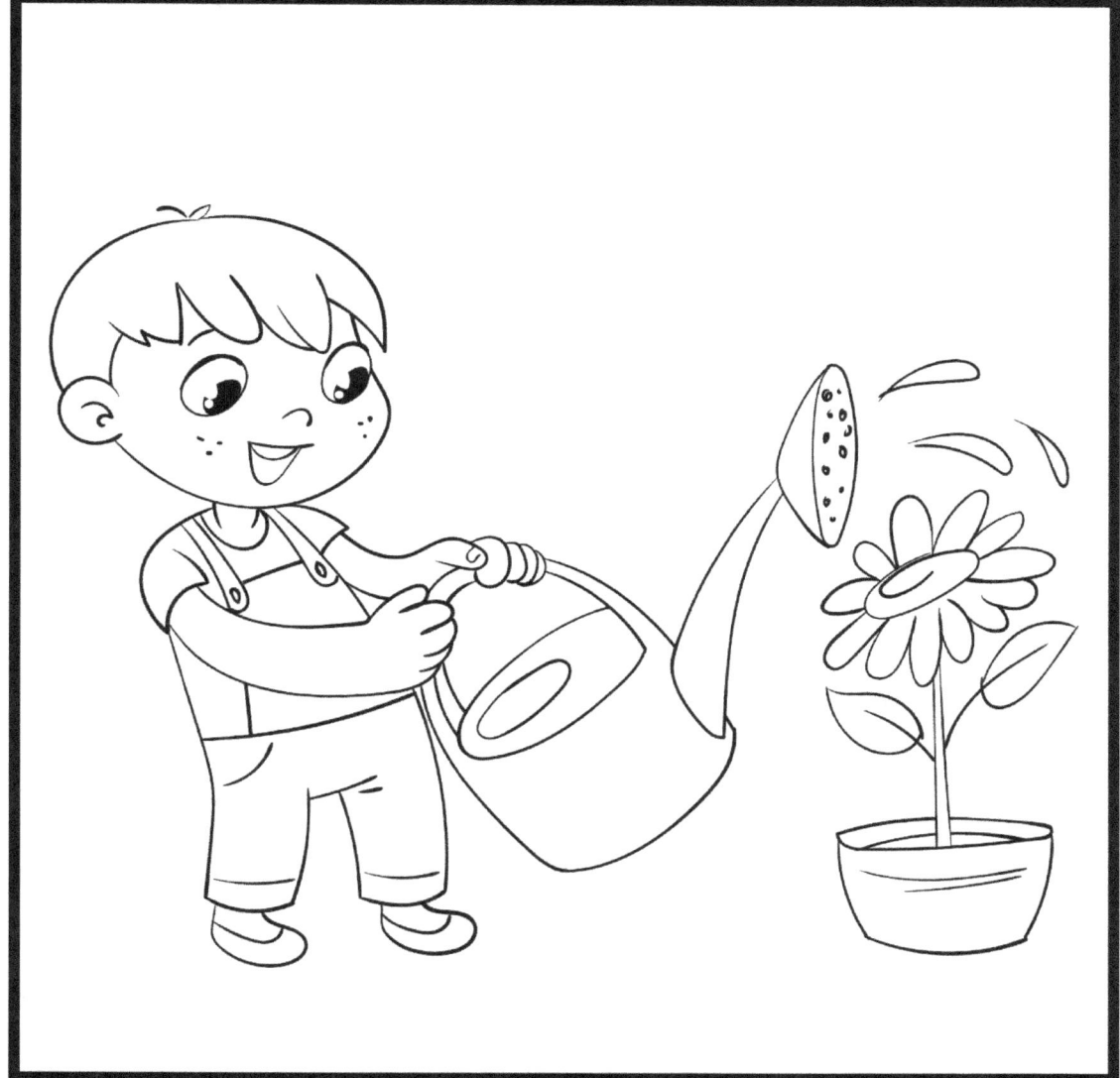

note:

_____

_____

_____

JUNE 46TH

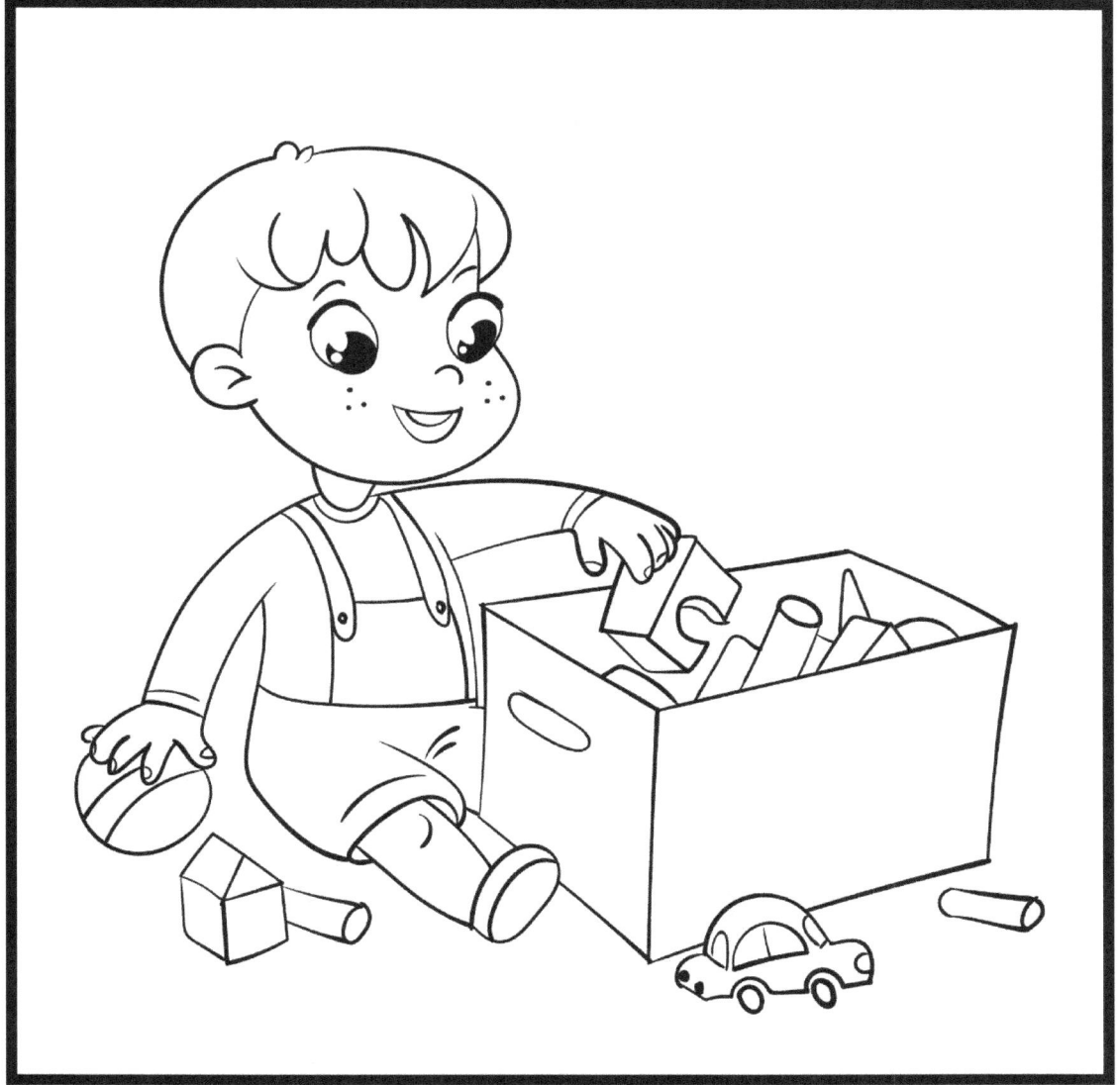

note:

_____

_____

_____

JUNE 47TH

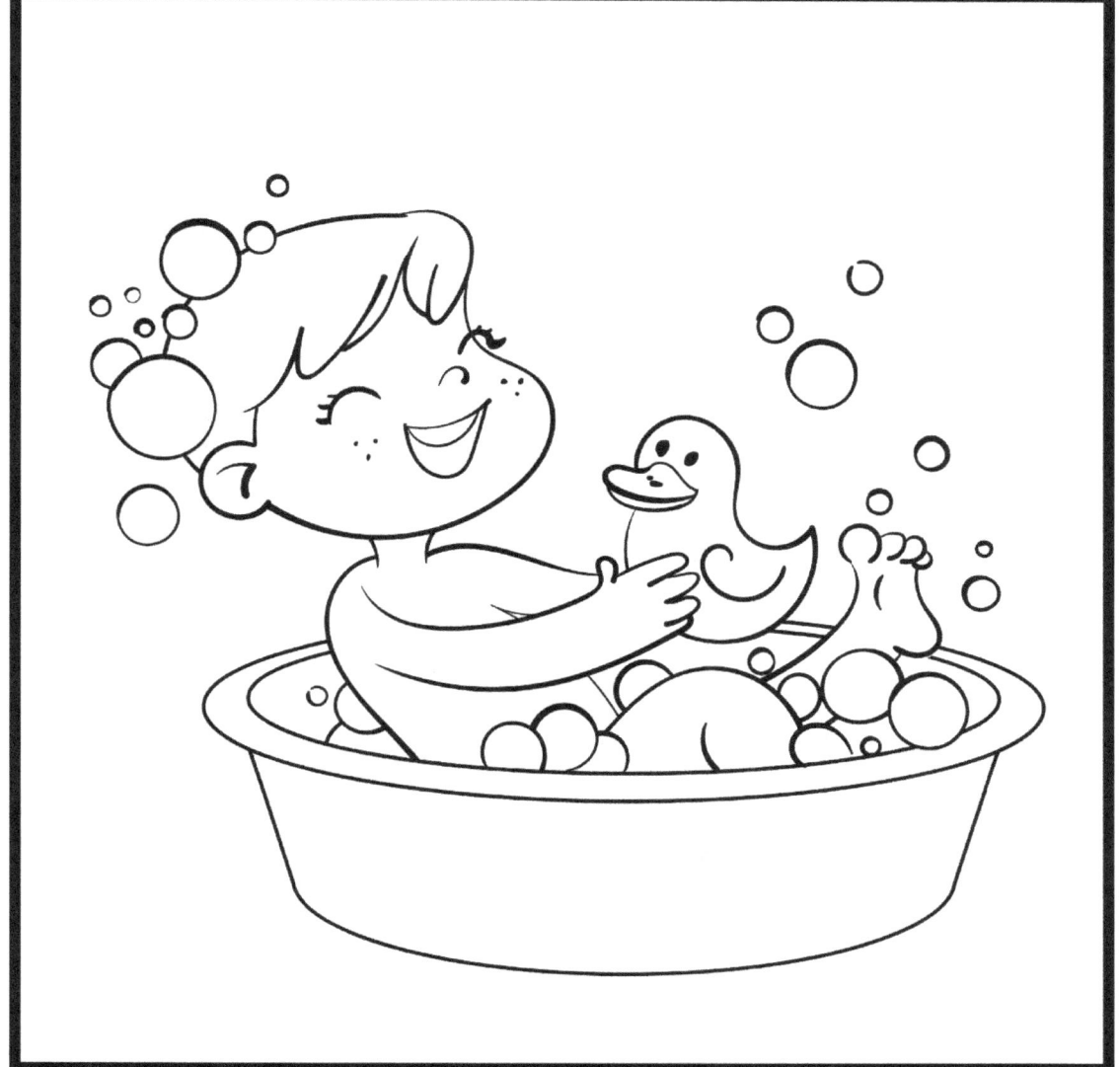

note:

_____

_____

_____

JUNE 48TH

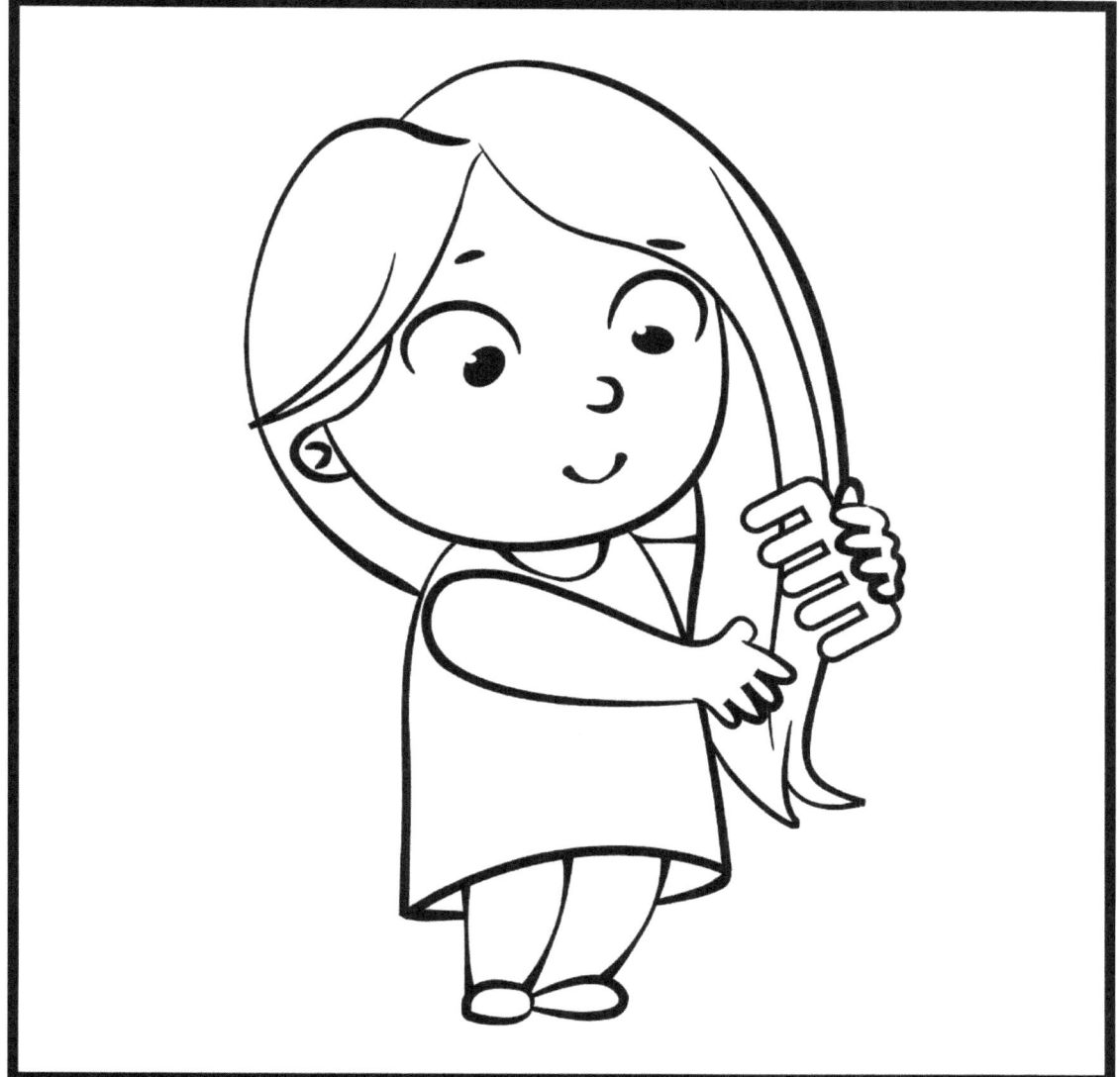

note:

_____

_____

_____

JUNE 49TH

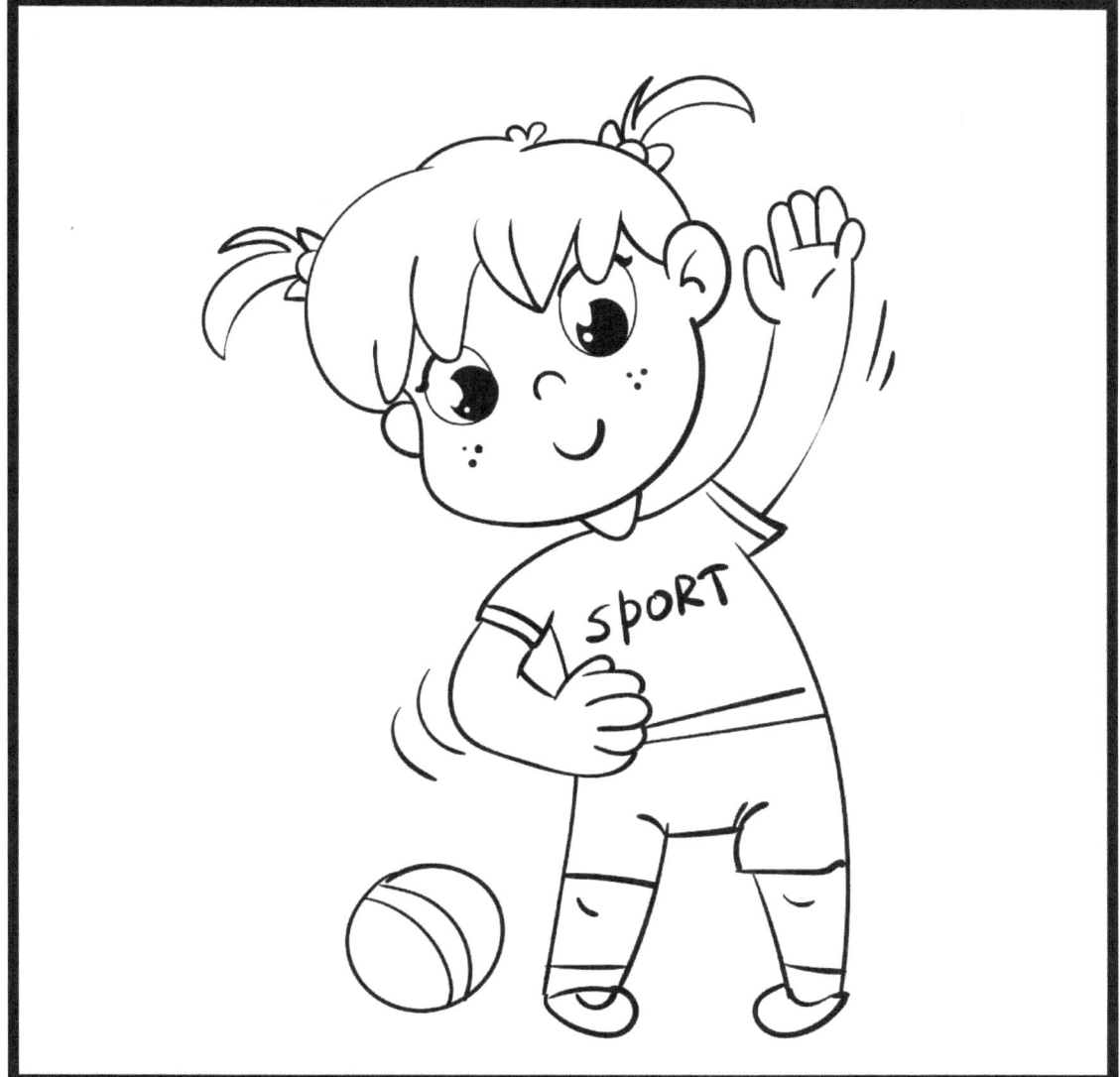

note:

_____

_____

_____

JUNE 50TH

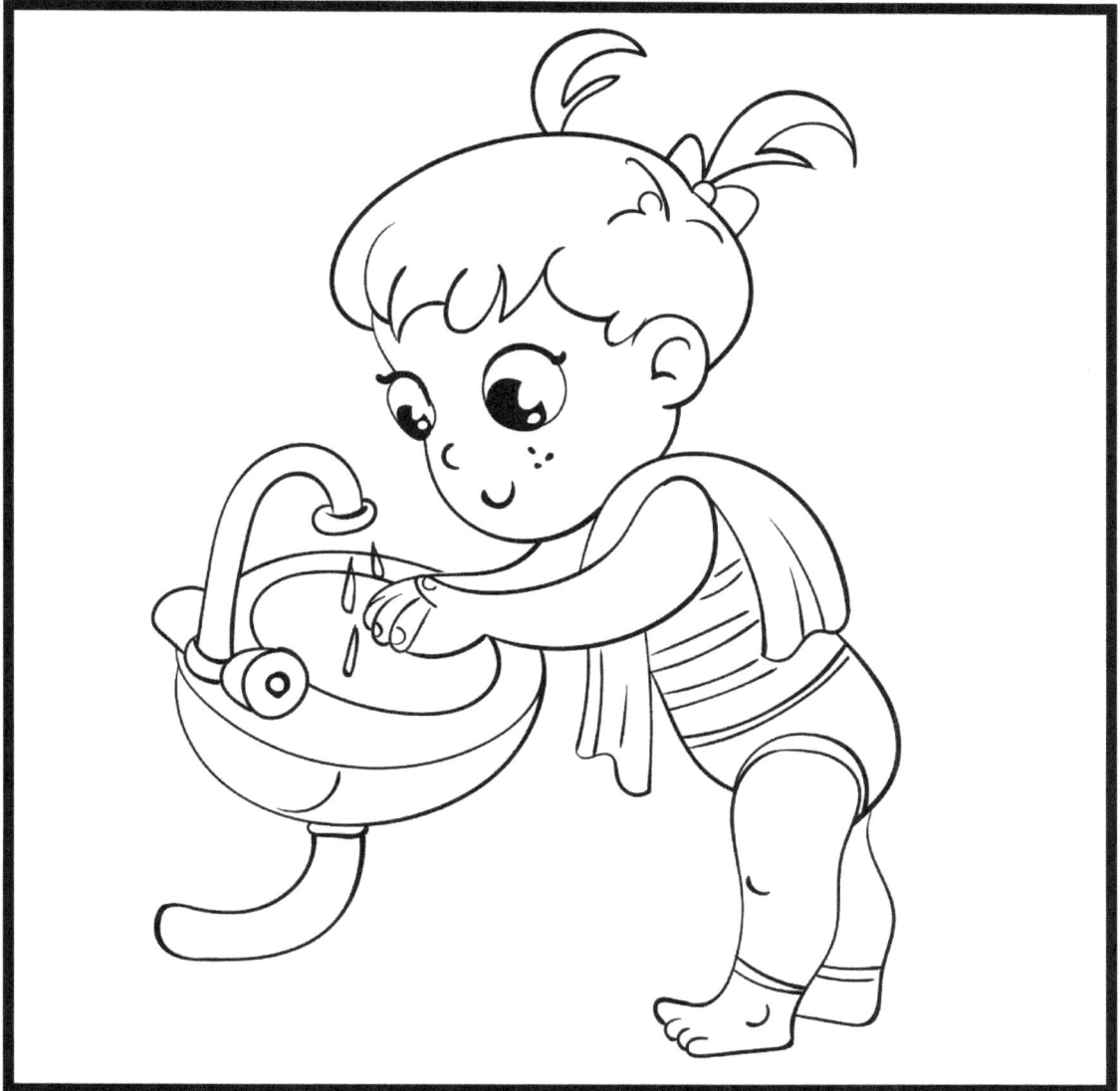

note:

_____

_____

_____